MONEY MATTERS & FINANCIAL EDUCATION

WHAT THEY NEVER TAUGHT YOU IN SCHOOL!

RALPH CARMICHAEL II

Money Matters & Financial Education

ISBN 978-0-578-27825-4 (paperback); 978-0-578-27838-4(hardcover)

Printed in USA by 48HrBooks (www.48HrBooks.com)

This book is dedicated to my Dad, who encouraged me to never take no for an answer, to go after my dreams despite what I have or didn't have, and never be average! He instilled in me nothing is impossible; it may take a great deal of work and effort, but anything can be achieved.

And to anyone seeking an increase in financial literacy, those wanting to-the-point guidance, and anyone determined to achieve financial freedom.

Before You Start This Book...

A quick word about the SELF-ASSESSMENT Pages:
There is a Self-Assessment at the end of each chapter of this book.
These are included to emphasize and help you personally apply
the messages of this book to your life.

"If you want something you've never had, you must be willing to do something you've never done."

— Thomas Jefferson

"Patience, persistence, and perspiration make an unbeatable combination for success."

— Napoleon Hill

The Self-Assessment pages are included to inspire you to read, understand, and implement the concepts of this Book and make changes accordingly.

Contents

Introduction

I started my first business back in the summer of 1998. In just a few short weeks I managed to acquire several yards in my neighborhood and in those surrounding it. I went on to gain contracts with a few small businesses that allowed me to keep their grounds cut. Imagine being a young kid like me — bringing in tons of money each week and being able to buy just about anything I wanted at the time — attempting to handle something I wasn't even fully aware of how it worked. Over the next couple of years, I went on to work various jobs in construction, warehousing, logistics and inventory, a few call centers, and even a popular baby store at the time. As I progressed through these jobs the desire to be in control of myself, my time, and the amount of money I could make, like I used to in my younger days, stayed constant in the back of my mind making me unhappy on any job I would choose.

After years of dealing with the rat race, chasing a check week to week, I decided to step back out and put some of the skills I'd gained along the way to use. I started writing business plans, handling business incorporations, doing a bit of business consulting, and became a notary. The money I made previously was nothing compared to the financial world I'd tapped into. I had all the latest cars, a nice home, traveled internationally, and a group of so-called friends along for the ride. Although it seemed I was on top of the world, and had everything a person could possibly want in life, I lacked the knowledge to sustain the life I'd obtained. As a result, I ended up with barely anything, my credit was terrible, I owed tens of thousands to the IRS, I had no savings or assets, and was left trying to figure out where I went wrong. My entire life I was working for money rather than assets for continued cash flow. I knew I had the money, but I never prepared for the future, and I certainly did not lay the proper foundation necessary to keep me financially free.

The world requires that you have good credit and pay your taxes each year, however they never explain how it all works. Like most people, I was never taught much of anything about the key aspects of finances at home or in school. As a result, I ended up like the majority of people, in debt with bad credit and no way out in sight. Most of us grew up with parents who did not fully understand money or the basic aspects surrounding it, even if they made a decent wage. School taught us to take tests and regurgitate information but never how to actively process information and problem solve. Ultimately school teaches you to be an employee working for wages, but doesn't prepare you to properly manage your money, start/run a business, nor inform you of the tools available to ensure you keep more of the money you make.

This book is not a memoir of my life story nor is it a manual on how to get rich quick. The principles of this book are intended to help you avoid making the same mistakes I made in life, or to recover from them if you have already fallen victim to the pitfalls of lacking a proper financial education. What you are about to read is fundamentally my playbook.... You'll learn the importance of structuring your taxes to your personal situation so that you get the maximum value out of your money. I'll teach you tricks and tactics that I used personally to eliminate debt, properly budget money, and identify a financial institution that will benefit you in the long run. I'll not only challenge your thoughts on credit cards, but also show you the many ways they can benefit you when used correctly. I'll delve into the aspects that affect your credit so you can better control your scores. And, you'll learn where to start when it comes to investing and better understand the elements of car and home buying.

There are people who utilize this knowledge every day to keep a leg up on everyone else, so you might as well be one of the people enjoying a financially stable and financially free life. After all, if a kid like me could build a successful life, have it all fall apart then successfully rebuild it (my credit scores are in the 800's, the bank cares if they keep my personal and business accounts, I have top tier cards that I can purchase anything I want on, my money works for me and my assets pay for the things I enjoy) without being born into an environment that properly prepared me for dealing with the aspects of financial education, then anyone has a chance. Remember there is no point in making money if you can't keep it.

Let's get started!

Starting with the Basics

Money and its Value

Our money used to have a real worth/value to it. President Nixon changed this in 1971 when he took our money off the gold standard. This means all our money is no longer backed by anything substantial which is why wealthy people value assets more than they do actually money.

Money is "nothing". The trick in life is to make enough "nothing" so that you can go out and buy "something" (real estate, stocks, bonds, start a business) that makes you more "nothing" that allows you to buy more "something".

This is why wealthy people often speak of cash flow because money is supposed to flow, keep moving, in order for it to be used properly.

Education as it Stands

While education is a must and as humans, we must never stop learning, one thing you will never learn in school is financial literacy.

Financial literacy can be defined as the ability to use knowledge and skills to make effective and informed financial decisions for a lifetime of financial security

Truth is, school in its current state only prepares you to be an employee; but to reach areas beyond this, or even sustain monetary gains of a high salary, you must increase your financial literacy to understand how money works.

Types of Income

- ***Ordinary income*** is income that employees and small business owners make. Small business owners are included here because many own a job, not a business because it can't operate without their active participation.
- ***Portfolio income*** is generated from investments, capital gains, interest, and dividends. This source is not earned through regular business activity.
- ***Passive income*** is generated from sources that do not require you to be actively involved such as multi-family properties, retail spaces and rental house managed by an external company

Asset or Liability

In simple terms, if it puts money in your pocket it's an asset, if it takes money away then it's a liability.

Your Perspective

Truth is many people remain in poverty because of their habits, mind set and lack of financial knowledge. Even if you gave everyone you know a million dollars, many, if not all, would be broke in a short period of time. Money seems to solve the issue on the surface, but it is the bad financial decisions that dig you in a hole and keep you there.

Many of us were raised by people who lacked financial literacy, so by default we lacked the necessary tools we needed to properly navigate the financial world. Statements like "go to school, get a job", "Work hard, then retire" and most of all "I can't afford it" are common. This way of thinking immediately keeps your brain from working out a solution or coming up with other possibilities; in many cases, you are your own worst enemy and it starts in your mind.

Discipline & Self Control

Having money, assets, and access to anything you could imagine sounds like a dream, but it means nothing if you lack the discipline necessary to handle it.

In all that you do, controlling you, your thoughts and actions is a necessity. For example, many people end up in tons of debt because they lack the self-control to not overspend on a credit card, or get things outside of their financial reach. Once in a sea of debt, those same people lack the discipline to properly budget, and eliminate the debts they've made because it does not fit the time schedule they have in mind; but getting started would be a far greater benefit than doing nothing at all.

Even with real estate and stocks you must be disciplined enough to do your due diligence so that you are aware of the risks and returns. You can't just jump into endeavors without doing the proper groundwork; the bigger the reward you are seeking generally means the greater upfront work that must be done. If you were going to build a home, or even a shed in the backyard, the foundation necessary to accommodate this building is minimal. Conversely, ***if you were building a skyscraper/high-rise, then you first must dig down deep and pour a substantial foundation to support the structure. This applies to every aspect of your life, if you are going after something great, the groundwork has to match that.***

Taxes: Facts You Should Know

There is a long-standing debate on why the rich seem to always get away with paying less taxes than those of lower income levels. Truth is, the harder you work, the more taxes you will pay because the government always wants their cut.

The reason rich people tend to pay less in taxes is because unlike an employee whose income is directly taxed, and generally their only source of income, the rich have assets that make them money. The government just wants taxes. They don't care who pays them, so they give business owners a break because there is no reason to go after them so hard. Because of them "creating jobs" they also create new streams of taxable income for the government in the process. The government offers all sorts of incentives, stimulus packages and perks to businesses for simply doing what they want done.

Corporations are taxed differently than an individual; "how" you make your money and "where it goes" determines how the government taxes the money, if at all

At the end of the day, employees will always pay more in taxes than small business owners, large business owners (hundreds of employees), and investors. The highest taxed income is earned income, the second highest is portfolio income and the lowest, sometimes not at all, is passive income.

When it comes to real estate, you get tax benefits such as depreciation (deduction received over time for the cost of the property), amortization (deduction for the cost of borrowing money like fees and interest) and appreciation (your property increases in value). With real estate, if you choose to invest your capital gains (profit from sale) into another property, you can use the "1031 exchange" method to possibly avoid taxation altogether.

O. P. M.

Other People's Money is a notion that keeps the wealthy where they are. This can come from loans, credit cards, lines of credit and even revenue generated from a piece of real estate. For example, if I owned an apartment complex and used some of the money to pay for another piece of property, I just used the money other people worked to get for my personal gain

401(K) - Ira Vs Roth 401(k) Roth Ira

There are several retirement accounts. These two are just mostly discussed. To determine which is right for you will depend on your current financial position, where you plan to be once this account reaches maturity, and how you would like to be taxed.

- A retirement account is just that, an account. However, what makes the money grow is what the funds in that account are used to "invest" in, such as gold and silver.

- In the simplest terms, with a 401(k), you put your money in untaxed then when you remove it later the funds are taxed. Most people under this system are told that their income will go down after retirement.

This notion assumes you will be poor, making no real money when you're older, and that will be the driving factor to lower your tax bracket. In some cases, you place money in, and your employer matches your contribution.

- IRA stands for Individual Retirement Account. In simplest terms with a Roth IRA, your money is taxed before it goes in. When the account reaches maturity, the taxes have already been paid so it can grow tax free.

Quick Tip #1: These accounts typically use a single asset class when investing your money, so if that one asset type (let's say stocks) were to fail, then you lose. Investing in several asset classes allows you to still have access to money and make money even if one of the others fails or isn't doing so well. Additionally, if you choose to have your money taxed later you are not sure today of what that tax will be; it could be reasonable, or record breaking high, further cutting into your profits. If you choose to be taxed up front, understand that the employer matched contribution will still be taxed at the end like the traditional retirement accounts, and you will be responsible for FICA taxes regardless of if you choose to be taxed up front or defer it.

Quick Tip #2: A 401(k) was never meant to be your primary means upon reaching the retirement age. While this method is better than wasting your money on things you don't need, and better than simply saving your money, it would be wise to have this working along with other investments so that you are not fully dependent on it.

Quick Tip #3: 401(k) accounts come with a lot of fees that most people are unaware of which also cut into your future profits. For example, the account must be managed on the other end, and those people make money off investing your money. If you try to pull your money out early, then you are hit with other fees and penalties. Also, while being an investor does come with several tax breaks, many of those breaks don't apply to your retirement account.

Quick Tip #4: There may be other options available to you when it comes to structuring your retirement account. Many people do

> not know about possible alternatives because they never ask. Your employer match is essentially them matching your investment. It may be possible for you to get your employer to match your investment in something else (like index funds) that you have more control over (and come with significantly lower fees) if you feel that you could successfully manage your own investments.

Banking

Saving should always be done with a purpose (such as making major purchases, preparing for emergencies, to invest, or to have six months of expenses set aside). Simply saving to leave money forever is foolish. As previously stated, money has no value these days, is no longer backed by the gold standard, and is essentially just a number in a computer. This means you will end up having an account full of nothing that you could be using to invest and acquire tangible assets that have more value than the money sitting in an account.

Bankers favor debtors over people that save. This is because when you save, the bank must pay you interest on your money. So, in their eyes you are a liability because you take money, no matter how minuscule it may be. Debtors are more favorable because they pay interest to the bank on loans. Ultimately, they put money in the bankers' pockets.

Be mindful, life is a game. So in the same way banks don't favor savers, it is viewed positively when you have money in reserve and typically keep a high daily average balance, because it shows you are making smart financial decisions. Additionally, because our banks run on what's called the fractional reserve system (essentially, they are only required to keep a fraction of the total reserves on hand and can loan the rest), they typically give checking accounts away free so that you will put your money in and allow them to make money on your money. There is no clear line here. It is a love-hate relationship with banks. They favor debtors, but don't like you with a ton of debt. They would rather not pay you any amount of interest on your money, but prefer you to have reserves.

Taxes Simplified

What Does That Mean?

The following is a list of terminologies you may come across when dealing with your taxes. Many of these terms can be defined several ways, but I'll give the most basic in order to establish a good foundation.

- Gross Income: The total amount of money that you make over a specific amount of time (before taxes).
- Net Income: The amount of money you actually take home (after taxes).
- Internal Revenue Service (IRS): Responsible for the enforcement of income tax laws and federal income tax collection.
- Adjusted Gross Income (AGI): Your gross income minus adjustments.
- Adjustment: Also known as Above-The-Line-Deductions, is a deduction (like a loan interest payment) that the IRS allows you to subtract from your gross income.
- Exemption: Can be classified as personal or dependency, such as a child or family member you are responsible for. These help to reduce the amount of taxable income.
- Deduction: Also known as Itemized Deductions or Below-The-Line

Deductions. These typically come in the form of mortgage interest payments, charitable donations, or charitable giving when giving funds to an organization such as a church.

- Standard Deduction: These are used when an individual lacks itemized deductions, so the government has set aside a flat deduction that can be subtracted.

> **Quick Tip #1:** You can't choose both itemized and standard deductions, so calculate it out and go with the one that is greater.

- Earned Income: This refers to salaries, wages, tips, self-employment earnings.
- Tax Bracket: This refers to the rate (what percent %) at which your money is taxed based on what income range you fall into (i.e., $0–$9,225, $9,226–$37,450…etc.).

> **Quick Tip #2:** The proper deductions/adjustments can help to control your tax bracket, which will be important as you take the journey of increasing your financial literacy.

- Tax Credits: Unlike exemptions and deductions that lower your AGI, tax credits directly lower your tax payments.
- FICA Tax: Money that is taken out of your check to handle social security, retirement, and Medicare.
- Filing Status: This determines the rate at which you are taxed.
- Single Filing Status: If you are unmarried, legally separated from your spouse (divorce, separate maintenance decree), or don't qualify for the "other" status on the last day of the year this is for you.
- Married Filing Jointly Filing Status: You and the person you are married to (spouse) agree to report your combined incomes and deduct your combined allowable expenses.

- Married Filing Separately Filing Status: You and the person you are married to (spouse) agree to file separate returns. This can be beneficial because in some cases you may pay less tax than if you filed jointly. Also, some people just prefer to only be responsible for their own taxes.

- Head of Household Filing Status: With this status there are requirements you must meet. You must be unmarried or considered unmarried on the last day of the year, you must have paid more than half the cost of keeping up a home for the year, a qualifying person must have stayed in the home with you for more than half the year except for temporary absences, such as school or dependent parents that do not live with you.

- Qualifying Widow(er) with Dependent Child Filing Status: This filing status has a lot of "what if's" associated with it, so to ensure that you are following the guidelines and that you qualify, consult your tax professional or call the IRS directly. The year they (the spouse) passed away, whether you are remarried, how you previously filled, etc. all play a part in whether the IRS will allow you use this status.

- W-2: The form that employers must submit to the IRS, and the employee at the end of the year, which serves as an official wage and tax statement that details the year-to-date (YTD) wages earned, and what taxes (social security, Medicaid...etc.) were withheld.

- 1099-MISC: This is like a W-2, except these are for what the IRS considers an "independent contractor". With a W-2, your taxes are paid as you earn wages. With a 1099-MISC, you have a collective report of the wages earned, and are responsible for paying the necessary taxes on those wages when you file your taxes.

- Self -Employed: Individuals who claim to be self-employed are treated as independent contractors because they are not employees of a specific company.

What Does That Mean?

Unearned Income: This refers to income that came from investments or interest from an interest-bearing account that you have money in.

Dependent: A child or qualifying child or relative (not the taxpayer or spouse) who entitles you to take advantage (claim) the dependency exemption. Dependents can file their own tax returns.

> **Quip Tip #1:** If you are not sure if you need to file a tax return, the IRS provides online tools that can help assess your situation and will determine if you meet the requirements necessary to file, or if you fall short of the threshold (amount earned or requirements) and do not need to file.
>
> **Quick Tip #2:** Be aware of your tax bracket because it can help you make better decisions when dealing with your credit. The federal brackets are 10%, 12%, 22%, 24%, 32% 35%, and 37% depending on your income range.
>
> **Quick Tip #3:** Be aware of deductions and credits that no one mentioned that you may be eligible for. There are tax breaks for college education costs, child adoption costs, childcare (and similar costs), losses you may have taken when selling stock, property taxes on real estate, and for people who fall below certain adjusted gross income levels. The list continues, so it is important to research and dig into all the possibilities because everyone is different, and you may miss something by simply doing your taxes like everyone else.
>
> **Quick Tip #4:** You do not need to pay someone to do your taxes because the program they use is the same one you would use at home. The program literally tells you line for line what numbers to enter in. Conversely, if you choose to do so, make sure it is someone who understands taxes and the way they work so that your filing experience is tailored to your needs and qualifications. If you are going to pay someone, it should be for their expertise on how to best structure your filing, not just for the ease of someone else doing it.

The W-4 (Federal Side)

W-4: Better known as the Employee's Withholding Allowance Certificate. Simply put, this is the form you fill out whenever you get a job. This form determines how much the employer will withhold from your check each pay period.

You will need to enter your full name, social security number, full current address, and filing status.

Following this you will see lines 5, 6, 7, and the date.

- On line 5, the higher the number is in this box, the less tax will be withheld from your check. Understand the government always gets their money, so paying less upfront does not always mean you won't pay more later; situations vary.

- On line 6 is where you can choose to have additional taxes withheld from your paycheck. This can help you decrease or eliminate the amount you owe in the future.

> Quick Tip: A large refund could be an indication that you are paying far too much in taxes, and you might need to adjust the taxes withheld, so that you can enjoy that money during the year instead of just once a year.

- On line 7 if you indicate "exempt" this means no taxes will be withheld from your checks. There are several rules that apply, so check them and be sure the route you choose to take is beneficial to you, and you do not end up with a large tax debt because you wanted to avoid taxes during the year.

- The date line is important because if your tax situation changes you can refile a new W-4 at any time. Do not think once you sign and date this, that's the end of the process. Although, in terms of taxes, you should play around with the numbers just for fun. Make changes if you have a child, get married, buy a house, take a pay cut, get a raise, or if you only work part of the year...etc.

The A-4 (State Side)

Depending on the state you live in there is another form that indicates how you are to be taxed with regards to the state. These rules generally vary by state, so it is important to identify how your state handles taxes. In some cases, an individual can work in more than one state and must follow the taxation guidelines of each. For example, in the state of Alabama they have an A-4.

A-4: Better known as the Employee's Withholding Exemption Certificate. Simply put, this is another form you fill out, in all that tax paperwork, whenever you get a job. This form determines how much state income tax to withhold from your check each pay period. Similar to the federal forms, you need basic information along with whether you plan to be exempt, and so on.

> **Quick Tip:** Many of these forms change, or are revised, from time to time, so it is imperative to stay on top of these changes. This is an important component of your financial literacy because it helps set your foundation in understanding taxation. There is no point in making money if you can't keep it.

Form 1098-T

1098-T: This is the form that educational institutions must send to any student who paid any qualified educational expenses in the prior tax year. Qualified expenses can include any tuition, fees or expenses that are required for the student to be enrolled, or to cover any course materials the student may need to continue enrollment.

> **Quick Tip #1:** you may not receive a 1098-T form if you are currently enrolled in courses that do not offer academic credit, if you are classified as a nonresident alien student, if your qualified tuition and fees were waived, or if your qualified tuition and fees were completely covered by scholarships.

You are not required to report your 1098-T unless you plan to claim an education credit on your taxes. If you plan to report this form, be aware that if your grant/scholarship amount located in box 5 is more than your tuition amount in boxes 1 and 2, then that excess money may be treated as taxable income when you file. While every situation is different, in most cases, tax credits can be more favorable than deductions.

> **Quick Tip #2:** There are several tax credits related to education like the Lifetime Learning Credit and the American Opportunity Credit. Be sure you are aware of credits that may be available to you whether you are the student or filing one on your return.

Form 1098-T will have all the basic information like your name, address, and so on. As well as some basic information on your institution. In addition, this form has 10 boxes with various information.

- Box 1: Your institution reports the total amount paid by you for qualified tuition and related expenses. The amount will be less any reimbursements or refunds made for that calendar year. This amount is not reduced by the information in box 5.

- Box 2: This is a reserved box used to indicate the amount billed to you for qualified tuition and expenses. This box may not always reflect what you actually paid so you want to have other records ready because that is important when calculating credit and deductions.

- Box 3: This a reserved box where your institution can indicate whether it is reporting that your status is "paid" or "billed".

- Box 4: Your institution reports any adjustments made during the previous year. This box is important because it can reduce any allowable education credit that you claimed in the previous year which could cause your tax liability for the refund year to increase.

- Box 5: This box shows the total of all scholarships and grants that your institution processed or administered for you. The amount of scholarships and grants may reduce the amount of education credit you can claim for the year. Be aware that this includes grants and scholarships not reported by your institution as well. Additionally, scholarships and grants are only tax free if you are pursuing a degree from an eligible institution and those funds are used to pay for qualified educational expenses. If you are no longer pursuing a degree, then the full amount of these funds is subject to tax.

- Box 6: This box indicates the adjustments made to the scholarships and grants you may have received for a prior year. If this figure affects the amount of allowable tuition and fees deducted, or education credit claimed in a prior year, then you may have to file an amended return for that particular year; This can be done using form 1040x.

- Box 7: This box indicates if any of the payments expressed in box 1 or box 2 are for the upcoming year.

- Box 8: This box indicates whether you are a part time (half-time) student. This means that you are carrying at least half the workload of a full-time academic workload as defined by your institution which must meet or exceed the standards set forth by the Department of Education under the Higher Education Act.

- Box 9: Your institution will report whether you are enrolled in a program leading to a graduate degree or graduate level certificate. This is important because some education credits and tax benefits are reserved for students who are at least part-time (half-time) pursuing an undergraduate level degree.

- Box 10: Your insurer will indicate the total amount of reimbursements or refunds of qualified tuition and fees they made. This is another box that may reduce the amount of education credit you can claim for the year, which could result in an increased tax liability for the year of the refund.

> **Quick Tip:** Forms, guidelines, and policies change, so do not be afraid to visit the IRS website if you feel any changes or updates may have occurred.

Taxes Self-Assessment

Take this time to identify your current situation. As you answer the following questions be honest, be detailed, and even make itemized charts to organize your answers. This information will help you determine where you are currently, and help you determine the steps needed to get where you want to be.

- Do you or someone else handle your taxes?
- Are your taxes current?
- Do you even need to file a tax return?
- Do you have any outstanding tax debt or liens?
- If so, have you established a suitable payment plan?
- Do you have a good understanding of taxes?
- Does the person you trust to do your taxes fully understand taxes?
- Are you getting all of the deductions and credits you qualify for?
- Are you paying too much in taxes each pay period?
- Which tax bracket do you fall in?
- Do itemized or standard deductions work best for your situation?
- Was your W-4 filled out correctly the first time?
- Are there beneficial changes to your W-4 that you could make?
- Are you showing enough taxable income?

Personal Finance

Budget Basics

To make this as simple as possible, a budget tracks where your money is coming in from, and where it went. Without the basic knowledge of budgeting, you will never be able to properly maintain your money, which is critical when it comes to obtaining and keeping wealth. Most people think that wealthy people spend money every day without a care in the world; they may not clock in to a nine to five, but their money becomes the job. You have to keep track of it and monitor how it flows.

> **Quick Tip:** On the journey to building wealth, one key factor that separates the wealthy from the poor, and middle classes, is that the average person has a job, and that income is responsible for paying the bills and expenses. The wealthy obtain assets that not only put money in their pockets but pays their bills. This would not be possible if they did not first understand the simple basics of personal finance like budgeting. As previously stated, the foundation you lay today affects what you plan on doing in the future.

Many people look at a budget as a restrictive tool that forces them to eliminate fun activities and prevents them from doing what they want. As your financial literacy increases, you will see discipline is a key factor.

A budget allows you to account for every dollar that you come in contact with so that you are able to eliminate unnecessary expenditures, then re-allocate those funds to other areas where they can be better utilized.

You have to understand the difference between a need and a want. Many people get in trouble here because they often place wants in the needs category, which leads to funds being spent unnecessarily.

How To Start A Budget

Everything you do must have purpose and reason so that you don't just initiate healthy financial habits but stick to them long term. Many of us were not necessarily bad at certain subjects in school, we just saw little to no real-world application which made us not really care; be honest here. The first step in a budget is determining why you want to budget in the first place.

Start by identifying your personal financial goals. What is it you are trying to do exactly? This may be so that you can better handle your finances, you want to pay off debt, save for college, save for a vacation, or buy a house. No matter the case a budget will give you an overview of your finances so that you can determine the necessary steps needed to reach your goals. While doing this, make sure you are specific so that you will have a realistic goal to reach. Don't label it "vacation money" but rather "$2000 for dream vacation". This seems miniscule, but it will help you set an actual goal and better track how close to achieving it you are.

Setting realistic deadlines for yourself will help you better manage your resources and track how well you stick to the plans you make. Also, detail how much it will take (per week, per month, per quarter) to reach your desired goals.

> **Quick Tip:** Budgeting on your own is a simple task, but for those who have an extra individual in the mix, things can get tricky. You all are a team, so it is important that you are on the same page when creating a master budget to achieve shared goals. In an average setting, you all will not make the same amount of money, so the person bringing more may have to give a bit more to make the plan work. Talk it out extensively and make sure both of you stick to it.

You must know everything coming in, and what's going out. Be mindful, some bills may vary month to month, so you will have to track these monthly. Eventually, you will see a pattern and be able to gauge the average amount that bill will cost you. You can make this chart yourself or choose to download one of the many apps that help you keep up with what's coming in and going out. Also, many banks and credit card issuers provide services that will calculate pie charts to show the percentages each expenditure takes.

Be aware of irregular expenditures because too many can hurt you, and in some cases it's these expenses that are sources where extra cash can be found. This category is sometimes where people spend money they don't have and tend to create unnecessary debt. ***Events like major holidays, birthdays, vacations, and unexpected medical expenses all contribute to a large portion of needless spending.***

Budget Type

The most common budget type is referred to as a ***50-30-20 Budget***. Here the basic premise is to allocate 50% of income towards needs (food, gas, debt payments…etc.), 30% for wants (video games, vacations, entertainment…etc.) and 20% for savings. This is an approach that has worked for a lot of people, however decreasing the amount allocated for wants and savings can allow you to pay down debts faster.

The ***Zero-Based Budget*** stipulates that after you save a percentage, every other dollar is allocated to something. So, in the end your income minus the outflow will equal $0. This approach has worked for some, but it is restrictive. This budget type can help to avoid overspending if you have not yet mastered self-control when it comes to spending.

The ***Spend First Budget*** occurs when you decide to spend money, then save and allocate whatever is left.

The ***Save First Budget*** occurs when you have a set percentage that you want to save, and then spend whatever is left on wants and needs. This method is what many wealthy people believe in and refer to when they say pay yourself first. This is an advanced method, so if you are just starting out, save this one for down the road because it means if you save first, you must either have funds in place to cover everything, or create new income streams to do so; setting a good financial foundation will allow this to happen, so master the basics. You will need them at each level.

There are a ton of budget types with creative names, but the basic idea is to do what works best for your situation. No matter the road you decide to take, just make sure you end up at the desired end. In your plan you should be handling your bills, decreasing debts, saving a percentage with a purpose, and achieving the realistic goals that you have set; this is how you will know if your plan is effective or if it needs to be modified.

Debt: Getting in is Easy, Getting Out Requires Dedication & Discipline

Debt comes in many forms, and while some debt could arguably be considered "good", this section only focuses on the bad. Some of the most common types of debt are medical debt, student loan debt, traditional loan debt, credit card debt, and mortgage related debts. Debt can pile up for many reasons, whether it is due to job loss, attempts to supplement income where there are gaps, or you simply did not properly manage and spent more than your income could handle.

Getting Out

The ***Snowball Method*** is one of my personal favorites. With this method you document all your outstanding debts, smallest to the largest. You want to be making the necessary minimum payments on all your debt, but if you have extra funds, make larger payments on the smallest then move to the next one. Basically, if you have a $100 debt, a $500 debt and a $1000 debt and the minimum payments are $25 a month. Start sending in $50 a month on the smaller debt which will pay it off quicker. Once this is done DON'T run to the mall with the extra cash, take that $50 and add it to the next debt so now you are sending in $75 on that one until it's paid off. Lastly, with that extra money you can send in $100 monthly on the last debt paying it down faster.

The ***Avalanche Method*** works a lot like the Snowball Method, except you focus on paying off the debt with the highest interest rates first, and so on until you reach the debt with the lowest interest rate. The more debt you have, obviously the more money you will need to eliminate them. Many people have more free time than they think, and properly allocating your finances is just as important as properly allocating your time. Wealthy people often cite time as being a great asset and they typically have a tight schedule on how they use it day to day. Also, they tend to say their proper use of time helped them get where they are and stay there. If you find yourself having free time and getting out of debt is truly important to you, then you may want to pick up a second job or side hustle. With this extra money, you could pay down your debt even faster because it's money you did not have previously anyway so you wouldn't miss it by overpaying your minimum debt payments. Sacrificing in the early stages will help you tremendously down the road because once the debt is gone, it's gone forever (once you are out of debt don't make the mistake of going back. It didn't work for you the first time, so why repeat bad habits)

The ***Minimalist Approach*** to debt is to only focus on those things that are necessary. This is a tough restrictive method because you will have to give up the parties, trending clothes and electronics that you want, put that vacation on hold, and not eat out. With this method you allocate every single extra dollar outside of your needs (rent, food, gas, etc.) to paying down debt. As I continue to say, this will take self-control for you to pull it off, but if you can stick to it, a debt-free life is much better and comes with less stress.

> **Quick Tip #1:** This all boils down to how important getting out of debt is to you. As an adult, no one can make you do anything, so that means you are left dealing with the toughest person to persuade and control; yourself.

An old-fashioned approach to increasing your funds, and decreasing debt is to sell off things you don't need. This may sound a bit time consuming, and a bit crazy, but when it comes to paying off debt, every little bit helps.

> **Quick Tip #2:** Most debt comes with an interest rate, so the longer you let it sit out there, the more that debt will cost you. In addition, not paying debts at all is a terrible idea because then they hit you late fees and penalties. Those things destroy your credit.

I've mentioned negotiating several times, and here is no different. It may be possible to negotiate a lower interest rate on some of your debt so that more of your money decreases the principle. Additionally, it may be possible to negotiate your recurring debts to free up money such as cable, satellite, internet, car insurance, and even your rent if you have a good history with them. With debt, you must consider all possibilities and go after them because they may just work and free up money to eliminate debt.

Getting Out

An alternative to negotiating is to remove the debt/bill all together. With all the streaming services available today, cutting your cable bill or eliminating it all together is now easier. Aside from online resources, the library may have that book you wanted to buy, or that movie you wanted to see, and you can get it for free. These are just more small costs that add up over time. By cutting out a $110 cable bill, you now have that much more to pay off debt simply by moving your money around and better allocating it.

As you budget, look for areas where you waste money, like that gym membership that you haven't used in years, or other monthly dues that you barely utilize. Also, try to avoid impulse buying, especially in the grocery store. They are designed to make you spend as much money as possible, which is proven every time you go in for that "one thing" and come out with a basket full. If you have trouble controlling your spending then try only taking in enough cash for what you need, make a strict list, and only get what's on it, or take advantage of a delivery service that'll bring your groceries to you, and keep you out of the store all together.

Birds of a feather flock together. This is also true when it comes to making poor financial decisions that keep you from moving forward. This may not seem to fit in the subject of getting out of debt, but ***when you have made a conscious decision to get out of debt you can't let the poor financial decisions of others pull you back to where you started.*** If those around you don't have similar goals in mind for financial freedom and increased financial literacy then it may be time to surround yourself with people headed in the same direction, are already where you want to be, or you will just have to gain enough self-control to stick to your plan regardless of what others are doing.

A ***Balance Transfer*** can help with paying off debt faster. Now at first glance it just seems like moving debt around which won't help you at all, however some transfer balance offers come with 0% intro APR for a certain number of months. While this does not pay off the debt, it gives you an allotted amount of time to attack the principal balance head on and eliminate the debt quicker than you would have swimming in interest and debt. In addition, you may find a balance transfer where the APR following the 0% time period is lower than your original interest.

Monetary increases can come in the form of a raise, work bonus, an inheritance, or that refund many people look forward to every year. When extra money presents itself, this is the time where you can tell if your mindset will lead you to being wealthy or keep you poor. There are a lot of people with high incomes still living check to check because they never took the time to set the right foundation, gain self-control, and increase their financial literacy. The presence of more money does not mean go buy more useless stuff. It means get out of debt and use the money to create new streams of income ***(money is nothing, so you have to turn it into something of real value).***

Be smart in these situations. Use the money you did not have before to improve your life and overall financial situation, not to make it worse and dig deeper in debt. To be frank, looking rich while struggling to afford something you didn't need is not as smart as properly handling your money, being debt-free and rich. Even if your goal is not to amass large amounts of money, a "keeping up with the Joneses" mindset will always keep you poor and swimming in debt.

> Quick Tip #1: Often, people waste their tax refunds on unnecessary purchases (TV's, cell phones, cars they can't afford, car accessories, food, lavish trips, etc.) instead of handling business. The most common excuse is that they have waited on this money and deserve to do whatever they want with it and paying off bills, in their mind is wasting the money. Contrary to this belief, taking the entire refund and putting it towards debt is more beneficial than wasting the money on liabilities and other items that don't produce any income or positively progress your life. Again, this takes self-control and dedication to bettering your life and overall financial situation.

You often hear people say, "fake it 'till you make it". No, drop the expensive habits that deplete your funds and don't positively affect your financial health. Expensive habits can also be something that appears simple like smoking or buying lunch on your break every day. These seemingly small habits cost you more per month than you may know, which is why a budget is necessary so you can see your poor habits and understand how they negatively affect you; this is more money that could be used to eliminate debt.

One of the biggest factors that keeps people in debt, aside from poor decision making and mistakes, is the fact that ***most people just do not want to face their own financial reality.*** This is bad because you can't plan to eliminate something you do not have all the details on. Getting out of debt starts in your mind first. You must change the way you do things, or you will continue to get the same results. Face it head on, and fully assess your situation so that you can better plan on how to handle it. Even if what you discover is worse than what you originally thought, don't let it discourage you. Make a plan and stick to it. Starting is more beneficial than doing nothing at all. ***When I was faced with a difficult situation as a child, my dad would always ask me "how do you eat an elephant?" and I would reply "one bite at a time".***

> Quick Tip #2: People jokingly refer to their children as their "broke best friends", mainly because they don't pay for their needs or wants but you love them enough to do it for them. When you implement a budget so you can get out of debt, save, or just better control your finances, understand your kids are now on a budget too. It's impossible to stick to a budget and put extra funds towards eliminating debt when you don't pull back on unnecessary expenses when it comes to your children. Doing this now will allow for you to freely do even more down the road; it works out better for everyone.

If you plan to get out of debt or be wealthy, and stay wealthy in the future, then you better understand the power behind saying no. I mentioned doing only those things that are necessary, and when you are trying to eliminate debt, giving money to friends and family can be detrimental to your progress. ***If two people are in harsh waters, one can't save the other until they first stabilize themselves.*** It may seem hard or selfish, but you must look out for your well-being or you will never get to where you want to be.

Banking Basics

In order to lay the proper foundation to understand banking it is important to understand all the verbiage associated with banking.

- Bank: A bank is a financial institution (traditionally a physical building before the emergence of online outlets) where they transmit funds, lend money, hold money and some banks sell and trade securities.

- Credit Union: Unlike a traditional bank, credit unions are not for profit institutions. They are run by the members, or people hired by the members, and their primary focus is not on turning a profit. Outside of a few differences, they operate and carry out many of the same functions of a traditional bank.

- Bank Statement: This is an ongoing report of all account activities that include all deposits, withdrawals, and any recurring payments you may have.
- Available Balance: The amount of money in your account that can be accessed immediately.
- Automatic Bill Payment: An authorized recurring payment to a certain business or entity.
- Billing Cycle: The period of time between the issuance of bank statements.
- Canceled Check: These are checks that have already been endorsed, charged to the account, and been paid.
- Cashier's Check: Unlike a traditional check this check differs in that the funds are drawn from the account immediately, guaranteeing the check won't bounce.
- Debit: This is money that is taken from your checking or savings account.
- Credit: This is money that is put into your checking or savings account.
- Deposit: Funds (cash, checks, or coins) that are put into your checking or savings account.
- Debit Card: A card the bank issues so that you can access your funds electronically through an ATM machine. When you use your card to make purchases or withdraw cash, it is automatically debited from your account.

- Deposit Slip: Instrument where you indicate the amount of your deposit and what form it is in (check, cash, or coins).

- Direct Deposit: Where you automatically have funds deposited into your account from a source you have a stated agreement, such as your employer.

- Electronic Funds Transfer (EFT): this includes any funds transferred by electronic systems rather than through cash or checks.

- Automated Teller Machine (ATM): These are automated devices that allow you to do certain transactions outside of the bank such as make deposits, withdraw cash, receive information about balances, make loan payments and transfer funds between accounts.

- Foreign Transaction Fee: Costs that are charged for processing payments for overseas merchants.

- Insufficient Funds: When an account doesn't have enough funds to cover withdrawals, debits, or checks.

- Overdraft: When the amount of funds withdrawn from the bank (by check, auto-pay, etc.) is greater than what is available in your account.

- Statement Date: This can mean several things but here we will focus on its meaning when they close out for the period and produce a monthly statement. This is important because when going after certain loans, they look at the average amount of funds you have in your account. If you know this date, then essentially you can control what's shown.

Quick Tip: While a standard proof of funds letter can be written up, in some cases the statement can be used to show proof of funds when going after home loans or auto loans.

- Pending Transactions: These are transactions that have not been fully debited from or credited to your account yet. A debited pending transaction can "fall off" meaning that it may disappear from your recent activities and then later hard post to your account. Be mindful here and keep up with your balances because this is a major cause of over drafting.

- Personal Identification Number (PIN): This is a private set of numbers that allow you to access the functions of a debit card, credit card and sometimes used as an identifier when calling a financial institution.
- Annual Percentage Yield (APY): This refers to the amount of interest you will earn each year on funds you have deposited; the bank is paying you for keeping/using your money.
- Federal Deposit Insurance Corp (FDIC): This is insurance the bank has that covers funds that are deposited up to a certain amount ($250k per account).
- Beneficiary: This is the person who will receive the money from your accounts when you are deceased.

Which Bank?

When choosing a bank, you have to think about what you want out of the financial relationship and if that institution is able to do that. Here are a few things to consider.

- Annual Percentage Yield should be considered because if you currently have a substantial amount of money or plan to get there one day, how much a bank gives you in return for holding your money is important.
- Convenience: The financial institution you choose should offer a variety of ways for you to access your funds (mobile banking, number of ATMs, etc.), and they should have enough branches where you can access them directly from just about anywhere. Additionally, your bank should offer around the clock customer service in case you need extra assistance.

- Bank Fees: Some banks will charge various fees when it comes to holding an account with them, maintain a minimum balance, minimum debit card usage and account transactions, and for using ATMs that are not a part of their network.

- Banking Services: Your financial institution should offer other services to you to assist you with both personal and business dealings. For example, some banking institutions have a cap on the size of loans they can issue, so if your business requires funds above this range then that institution may not be the right one for you.

> **Quick Tip:** Do not always choose a bank that is beneficial to your current financial circumstances. Plan for the future and where you want to end up, because the longer you are with an institution the more time you have to build a solid relationship for the future. You should benefit just as the bank does.

Opening An Account

When opening an account with a financial institution they will need your name, address, birthday, and a form of government issued ID like a driver's license, social security card, or passport. If you are opening an account online, they may require you to mail, fax or bring in documentation.

Going into a financial institution is the best method because you will have the opportunity to ask questions, and see what the bank can do for you. See what tools they have available that can help you with budgeting, bill pay, financial monitoring, and what they have available to track and help you meet certain savings goals. We often limit technology to social media use, but it can do so much in terms of your finances so don't hesitate to ask what's available.

Personal Finance Self-Assessment

Take this time to identify your current situation. As you answer the following questions be honest, be detailed, and even make itemized charts to organize your answers. This information will help you determine where you are currently and help you determine the steps needed to get where you want to be.

- Do you currently have a budget?
- Does your budget include all the money you have coming in and going out?
- What three items make up the largest percent of the money you spend out?
- Can you identify areas where you can cut back and free up funds?
- Can you identify all recurring memberships, subscription, services, and products that you pay for monthly?
- What are your financial goals?
- Do you and your significant other have the same goals in mind?
- Are these goals realistic and what timeframe is set to achieve them?
- What is your total amount of debt?
- What makes up the largest portion of your debt?
- Are you currently repeating the same mistakes that got you in debt initially?
- What percentage rates do your debts hold?
- Do you have a checking or savings account?

- How much is currently in each account?
- Who do you bank with?
- Have you considered multiple financial institutions?
- What do they offer that is beneficial to your financial future?
- What type of relationship do you have with your financial institution?

Understanding A Secured Credit Card

Unlike a traditional credit card, a secured card is backed by your money and not the bank. You can get a secured card from your credit union/bank or you can go with a major issuer like Bank of America, Citi, Discover, or Capital One. The typical minimum security deposit is $200 (card limit).

- Most banks require you to put down how much you want as a limit plus an amount over that (based on your credit) (can be as much as 125%) in order to get the card.
- Some issuers will give you the card as long as you have the money, while some, even with the proper funds can still deny you. Research to determine how each bank operates.
- The majority of secured cards do not have an annual fee because they are meant for people with no credit or who are rebuilding their credit file.
- Secured cards typically do not offer the same rewards and perks as many of the traditional credit cards.
- You do not "stack" multiple secured credit cards like you do a traditional card because they are meant to build credit, get you in the game, and move on.
- Secured cards tie up your personal money which is another reason you do not want to get multiple; one is more than enough, but two is the limit if your credit is really poor.

- The issuer will generally "graduate" the card (change it to traditional card) anywhere from six months to a year depending on their system. After the "graduation period" (card switched to traditional card) you get the funds you put on the card back.
- Depending on the issuer (inquire before getting the card), some will simply change the card from a secured card to a traditional card without changing the card number and you keep your account history; conversely, others will remove the old card and replace it with the new card starting your account history over.
- Other regulations, rules and guidelines are issuer specific, and that information can be obtained from them directly

Top Reasons to Use a Credit Card Over Cash or Debit Card

- When using cash, it's instantly gone.
- If stolen, the cash is gone forever.
- If your debit card is compromised or stolen, your actual money is gone.
- Using a credit card doesn't affect your actual money.
- If your credit card is stolen, or compromised your actual money is not affected.
- Credit card use allows your average daily balance to remain higher, thus giving the bank the perception that you aren't desperate for money.
- Credit cards help boost your credit score, and aid in maintaining higher scores, whereas cash/debit cards do not.
- Credit cards improve your credit by helping your utilization and average age of accounts.

- Credit cards allow you to report more positive payment history with things that otherwise wouldn't even count if purchased with cash.
- Many credit cards offer purchase protection (theft and/or damage insurance essentially).
- Many credit cards offer price protection (essentially price match).
- Most credit cards offer warranty protection (extended warranty).
- Most credit cards offer return protection (allows you to return stuff to them that is outside of a merchant's normal refund/return policy).
- Credit cards offer rewards points, cash back opportunities and/or other rewards and perks that can't be achieved with cash or debit cards (free trips, free tickets, airport lounge access, cash back, rental car perks, hotel status, etc.).
- Credit cards are essentially a personal line of credit at your disposal so there is no need to beg the bank for what you already have.

Proper Ways to Utilize Your Credit Card

- Avoid interest and pay your card in full each month.
- Know your statement date so that you can properly track when that card reports to the credit bureaus.
- Use your credit card like your debit card; only spend what you actually have.
- Never make purchases just because the funds are available to you.
- Never make extra purchases just to meet "minimum spend" (amount needed to obtain the card bonus when you initially get it).
- Keep your credit utilization at 10% or lower; some say 30% but that's too high.

- Only get cards that fit your spending habits and directly benefit you (cash back, travel, etc.).
- Pre-paying your cards (weekly/bi-weekly) can inspire the bank to increase your spending limit as well as increase your credit score over time.
- Pay attention to if a card has an annual fee or not, this is an expense you incur without ever using the card.
- Most places charge a certain percent to use a credit card versus cash or debit card. If the benefit (rewards/perks) of that charge does not outweigh the extra percent paid, then don't do it (points gained worth more monetarily than the percent paid).
- Determine the upgrade and downgrade paths of a card in case it becomes less useful to you, and you want to move up or down to a card the issuer has that suits your needs.
- Understand a credit card can carry a balance while a charge card must be paid off in full every month (unless it has a pay over time feature), but the goal is to NEVER carry a balance at all.
- Canceling a card affects your average age of accounts, so the longer it is left open (in good standing), the better effect it has on your credit score. Once your credit file is "thicker" then closing a card won't hurt you as bad.
- Good credit requires some form of "debt" to be actively paid in order for it to become high. So, several credit cards can be used to replace bad debt with debt you "control" and continue positive payment history.

What Interest?

To play the game of credit properly, you should never be paying any interest on your cards. Whether it is a charge card (which has to be paid in full every month, but some companies have a pay over time option), or a traditional card (that can carry a balance month to month as long as the minimum payment is met) paying the full balance eliminates the interest all together. Also, doing this saves you money, and builds better credit; it's a win-win situation.

Higher Limit Cards

The better your credit score the better chance you have of being approved for a card that comes with a higher limit. Income can also come into play depending on your situation. There are some cards that come with a minimum credit limit; for example, the Chase Sapphire Preferred comes with a minimum $5,000 limit and the Chase Sapphire Reserve comes with a minimum $10,000 limit. When going after cards like this, understand you have a better chance of being approved if your credit report shows that you have access overall to higher limits and can handle this much credit or more (if you want a card with a $5k limit then already properly managing $5k or more on your credit will increase the odds).

Charge cards like the American Express Platinum essentially come with no pre-set limit like a standard credit card. Cards like this focus on what's called "buying power". With this, the issuer looks at your buying patterns and your "buying power" depends on how much you put on the card and successfully pay off. There are all sorts of algorithms and mathematical equations that help the issuer determine this, but in simple terms, the more you put on it and successfully handle the more buying power the issuer will allow you to have. In some cases, larger purchases outside of your "buying power" can be approved with a simple phone call given you have a positive relationship with the issuer.

It's Levels to This

Not all credit cards are created equally. Each card comes with its own rewards, perks, value, etc. This primarily depends on what tier the card is on. In the world of credit cards, there are fundamentally five tiers that a card can fall under. Depending on if you see the glass as half empty or half full, you could argue that the tiers should be ranked 6 to 1 because 1 in the world of winning is best; however, you could argue the tiers should be ranked 1 to 6 because 6 is the bigger number and signifies going up like a staircase. I'm going to use 1 to 6 because it's easier to keep up with numerically.

Tier 1: At this level you have what is referred to as **Credit Building Cards.** This tier can help those new to credit establish positive credit with proper use and it can also be beneficial to those wanting to rebuild their credit and return to a positive standing. One example is a **Student Card.** In some cases, this type of card can be graduated to a more useful card down the road, but as the name implies you have to be a student. There are some cases where non-students got these cards.

Another example would be **Secured Cards:** Depending on the issuer this card can have an upgrade path to a more useful card, but it does require you to put up your own money initially.

Lastly **Subprime Cards:** there is no deposit required like a secured card and typically has little to no requirements but in the long run the card isn't very useful and lacks value due to the increase in costs to carry it; avoid these!!

Tier 2: At this level you have what I refer to as **Foundation Cards.** At tier one, you set the foundation for your credit as a whole, but here you are setting your card foundation in order to move on to better cards in the future. These cards do not have an annual fee, but still help you in terms of building your credit score. These cards do not require a deposit like many of those in tier one and at this level you can start getting cash back or other forms of card rewards. Additionally, while adding to your average age of accounts these cards cost you nothing, and as long as you use it at least once every six months on a minor purchase it will stay active.

Tier 3: At this level your focus is still maintaining positive credit, but you want to utilize that credit card foundation discussed previously in order to move on to cards that give you something in return. This way you can build credit by spending money on things you would normally, while being rewarded simultaneously. These cards typically do require an annual fee, but the value (benefits and rewards of the card) should off-set or eliminate that fee. For those who like to travel, this means if you have a card that has an annual fee of $95-$195, but it gives you an annual free night reward, the free night is valued higher than the fee, so you come out ahead before even considering the other benefits of the card.

Tier 4: At this level you get more benefits from the card (higher point multipliers, more points for minimum spend, better protections on purchases, etc.). However, these cards do require you to spend a lot more money (annual fees, minimum spend, overall spend before certain rewards are made available). Another benefit of these cards is they will likely come with larger point bonuses and if you use the card on purchases you were going to make anyway, then you do not have to make unnecessary purchases in order to meet the minimum spend (amount necessary in the first 3-5 months in order to get the points bonus). Another positive to these cards is many of them come with a downgrade path, so in the event the card is no longer useful to you or some life event makes it unaffordable, you can go back to a card with lower fees or no fees (this is a way to "recession proof" your wallet in the event your monetary situation shifts).

Tier 5: At this level the annual fees can range from $400 to $695. These cards can come with various combinations of higher multipliers (4x instead of 3x), travel credits, statement credits, airport lounge access, free night certificates, free weekend night certificates, complimentary status with brands like Marriott/Hilton/Hyatt, business credits, Uber credits, increased purchase/fraud protection, travel insurance, cash back on qualifying business purchases and the list goes on. While these cards do come with higher annual fees, minimum spends and sometimes spend requirements to obtain certain rewards. When used correctly, just like in the other tiers, you can effectively decrease or eliminate these increased fees. For example, if I have a card that has a $450 annual fee, but I get a $250 statement credit and other perks valued around $150, I now have an annual fee of $50 due to the value I received from the card. Specific examples of this would be the American Express Hilton Aspire card which comes with several benefits; one of the primaries being complimentary Hilton Diamond status which is their top customer status. When you add up the amount of money and stays necessary to reach this level, and then value all the benefits that you get with this status, the value far exceeds the annual fee on this card. The American Express Platinum and the Chase Sapphire Reserve give you priority pass, statement credits, travel credits, global entry credit and many other benefits that essentially eliminate the annual fee based on the amount of value you get back from the card. Lastly, if you are a current business owner or future entrepreneur cards like the Chase Ink Business Preferred has far too many benefits to list here, but having purchase protection, extended warranty benefit, being able to transfer the points to partners for other purchases, trip cancellation/interruption insurance and bag delay/ loss insurance if you travel can help to eliminate the annual fee.

> **Quick Tip:** Remember when utilizing any form of credit, to come out ahead you want to minimize or eliminate your interest. The same rule applies here, as you go through the different tiers your value and benefits should always be higher than what the card costs you so that the fees or minimum spends no longer matter because you get more back than what you put out. If it costs you $200 then you should be getting back more than $200 in overall value. In the game of credit, always play to win, always ensure you benefit, and always come out on top.

Tier 6: At this level these cards are **Invite Only Cards.** As the name implies you have to be invited to apply for this card by the issuer. Unlike other cards, you can't just go online or pick up the phone and apply for this card type. These cards can come with annual fees that range from $595 to $5000 and an initiation fee of $10,000 just to obtain the card. While there is a lot of speculation on these cards, the issuers do not put out specific information on how to qualify for these cards. Perhaps one of the most notable invite only cards is the "Black Card", officially named the American Express Centurion Card. It is rumored that you must spend, and pay off, at least $250,000 to $450,000 in order to be considered for this card. While the tier 5 American Express Platinum does come with a concierge line that you can use to get tickets to events, or gain entry to restaurants that are booked, the Centurion Card comes with an on-call personal concierge assistant that is there to help you out with just about anything you need. Some of the benefits of tier 6 cards can also be found in tier 5 cards. At tier 6, the limits are substantially higher or non-existent. Many of the perks are enhanced, but most of all these cards are a status symbol for all those that carry them.

Rules... Not Meant to be Broken

Whether you are applying for your first card or your fourth, there are a few rules to keep in mind as you embark upon your credit card journey. These rules regulate everything from how many cards you can get at a time to welcome offer eligibility. Please note that while some credit card rules stay the same, some are updated or replaced at the issuer's discretion. Each institution is different, but let's look at American Express and Chase Cards just to give you an idea of how institutional rules work.

American Express (Amex)

Because some cards come with welcome bonuses many people have come up with creative, yet punishable, ways to meet the minimum spend. Amex reserves the right to "clawback" points if you get your points by any means they deem inappropriate. For example, if you use your card to send large amounts of money to friends, then get the money back to pay the card off; if you purchase several gift cards then use them to pay your bill or cash equivalent purchases like Visa/Amex gift cards. All of these will raise red flags and your points could be taken from you, your card could be shut down and you could be blacklisted for such behavior.

If an issuer notices that you open cards and close them before twelve months this will send a red flag that you are possibly opening cards just to accumulate welcome offers.

Once in a Lifetime Bonus: After you have had any of the Amex products in the past or presently, you will not be eligible for that bonus again. So, if you had the Amex Everyday card and decided to cancel it, or you decided to upgrade/downgrade (product change) it for another card, you will not be eligible for another Amex Everyday card bonus in the future. An exception to this would be cards like the Amex Platinum that have many variations such as: Mercedes-Benz, Charles Schwab, Morgan Stanley, and other variations of the card. Because this card has different variations, you are eligible for the bonuses on each one.

Five Card Limit: Amex limits you to having only five of their credit cards at any given time. So, if you had 5 you would have to cancel one to open the new one. This rule does not apply to charge cards. They allow you to have as many of those as you would like (Amex Green, Gold, and Platinum). While this may vary, in most cases if you already have one Amex card, they will do a soft pull when approving you for new cards.

- 1 in 5 Rule: This rule dictates that you can only get approved for one new Amex card every five days and if you try to go over that you will be denied.

- 2 in 90 Rule: This rule stipulates that you can only be approved for two Amex cards every 90 days. So, if you decide to apply for a third card, understand you will be denied. (Note: This applies to credit cards, not Amex charge cards).

Chase

- 2/30 Rule: This rule stipulates that you can only have two applications every 30 days and anything above this will automatically be denied.

- 5/24 Rule: This is one of the most important credit cards rules to pay attention to because it can affect you if you plan on having multiple cards. This rule specifies that if you have more than five new credit cards in the past 24 months, that is from any issuer, you will automatically be denied for a new Chase card. (There are a few exceptions to this, but the main exception to this rule are the Chase Business Cards).

- 1/24 Bonuses: Unlike Amex, if you have a Chase Card, you are eligible for the bonus every 24 months. This means if you applied for a card in 2019 then decided, for one reason or another, to apply for another one then years later you would get the bonus again. (This doesn't apply to the Sapphire cards).

- One Sapphire Rule: This rule prohibits you from having more than one Sapphire Card; meaning you can have the Chase Sapphire Card, Chase Sapphire Preferred (CSP), OR the Chase Sapphire Reserve (CSR) but not all of them. The only exception to this is for people who had multiple Sapphire Cards before the rule came about in August of 2018.

- 1/48 Sapphire: With this rule you can only receive one Chase Sapphire Card Bonus every 48 months. If you got the bonus in 2019, then you would not be eligible again until 2023.

> **Quick Note:** There are other rules and guidelines out there that are credit card specific, but this list is to give you the foundation necessary to understand how the rules work, and how to make a plan that best suits what you are trying to accomplish. Always check the issuer website for updates on rules, and the way they handle transfers, upgrades/downgrades and reward eligibility.

SCRA / MLA

The Servicemembers Civil Relief Act (SCRA) and the Military Lending Act (MLA) have benefits that many servicemembers may not even be aware of.

There are several cards that come with high annual fees, but for servicemembers these fees can be avoided altogether. This means that servicemembers are able to enjoy the full benefits, credits and sign-up bonuses of some cards without paying the annual fee (American Express and Chase are most notable for this). If you do not anticipate getting the same value in these cards to justify the annual fee once you are no longer active (typically 15 months after active duty ends), then you can simply downgrade them to a lower annual fee card or one that does not have an annual fee at all.

Credit Cards Self-Assessment

Take this time to identify your current situation. As you answer the following questions be honest, be detailed and even make itemized charts to organize your answers. This information will help you determine where you are currently and help you determine the steps needed to get where you want to be.

- Do you currently have any credit cards? If so, how many?
- If you're new to credit cards, which one do you want first? Does it benefit you?
- How many would you like to have overall? Why?
- If you plan to get a secured card first, which one? Why?
- Do you have any charge cards?
- Which exact cards would you like to obtain? How do they benefit you?
- What is the total balance you currently have on your cards?
- Do you carry a balance and pay the minimum each month?
- Do you pay your cards off in full each month and avoid interest?
- What are the limits of each card?
- What percent of each card's limit are you utilizing currently?
- How is your payment history on your cards?
- Have you ever defaulted on a card?
- Have you opened or closed a card in the last three years? Why?

- What benefits (rewards points, cash back…etc.) do your cards give you?
- What tier do your current cards fit in?
- What tier would you like to achieve?
- How often do you utilize your debit card? Why?
- Can any of your cards be upgraded to better cards from the issuer?
- Can any of your cards be downgraded?
- Do any of your cards offer balance transfers? At what interest rate?
- Do you have a good relationship with your card issuer?

Factors That Affect Your Credit

Payment History – 35%

Do you pay your bills on time or are you a risk because you have a history of late payments, defaults, charge-offs, and other derogatory marks?

Credit Utilization/Amounts Owed – 30%

This refers to what percent of your credit limit you use each month (stay under 10% preferably). "Amount owed" refers to how much outstanding debt you have at the time, and how this can potentially affect your ability to repay a new loan or credit card. This also covers how much the monthly payment is to each debtor to determine credit worthiness and funds left available to pay new accounts

Inquires – 10%

These hit your credit when a lender or issuer does a "hard pull" on your credit to determine if you should get a new car loan, mortgage, or credit card (soft pulls don't really affect you).

These will decrease your credit score because they go hand in hand with average age of accounts; so, the more you have the worse the effect. Also, they stay on your credit for two years ("thin" files are hit harder).

Length of Credit History – 15%

This is what's referred to as the average age of accounts. Basically, how long have you had your accounts open and is that history positive?

New Credit

Applying for too much new credit can send a red flag to lenders that you are a high risk, may be up to illegal or unproductive practices, and you should be denied.

Types of Credit – 10%

- Having a variety of credit types shows you are a diverse borrower, which positively affects your score.
- Installment loans (fixed payments like car loans) (Report Monthly)
- Revolving Accounts/Debt (credit cards) (Report Monthly)
- Real Estate Loans (mortgages and home equity lines of credit)
- Open Accounts (Cell phone bills) (Only Report Negative Activity)

Why Does Credit Even Matter?

The fact of the matter is that if you have a poor credit history, you can pay more when you go to purchase a vehicle. If you decide to purchase real estate (personal or investment), you can be denied altogether even if you simply want to rent. Credit matters because in the end it will cost you more for having poor credit and save you money for having exceptional credit (lower interest rates, lower or no down payments, etc.). Additionally, while money can open several doors, credit can typically open those same doors with less money out of pocket making it a more important step than the money.

Ways to Build Credit

- Pay your bills on time and keep your debts low to non-existent.
- Pre-pay on your credit cards and loans, don't just wait for the bill to come out.
- Know your statement date/closing date (by doing this you can control what your issuer/lender reports to the credit bureaus thus being able to essentially control your credit increases). In short, if your card limit is $500 and you use $450 of that limit, when it reports you will hurt your score with high utilization. However, if you use that same amount or more throughout the month but make a payment before the card reports then essentially you hide your true usage and continue reporting low utilization which looks good to creditors.
- As previously discussed, a secured credit card is a good way for those with no credit, thin credit file, or in the stages of rebuilding credit. It allows you to put up the money to back the card then use it to gain positive reporting history; later you get those funds back.
- Similar to a secured card, some banks will allow you to secure (or "back") a small loan with your own money. With this method you deposit funds into an account, the bank places a hold on those funds to ensure repayment of the loan, and as a result you now have a positive payment history reporting to your credit.
- Being an authorized user is a great way to build a high credit score quickly. With this method a person with a great credit history (because someone with terrible credit won't help you at all in this situation) puts you on their account; Although in most cases the full responsibility of repaying the debt is on the original cardholder you get your own card, and you take advantage of the credit history they have already built. Some card issuers may want you as an authorized user to have the reported history start from the time of the new card being issued; in this situation it's either their company policy to do

so or they can be persuaded to grant full credit history of the card; it varies. (Side Note: if you are married and at least one of you has good credit you can make your spouse an authorized user and they benefit from the same card without applying for it personally; make sure you can trust them, and you all have a well thought out plan)

> **Quick Tip:** While this method is effective, be mindful that your profile matters more than your score. Additionally, once this tradeline is removed your score will drop and institutions respect primary accounts over authorized accounts.

Ways to Ruin Credit

- Miss payments or make late payments — If you can do auto pay, enable it and you will be fine.
- Maxing out your credit cards — This increases your credit utilization too high and makes you seem like a high risk.
- Applying for too much new credit at one time--This is tricky because a larger credit file and credit history, when done well makes for a great credit score but doing it too quickly and often can hurt you; monitor your credit and make calculated decisions based on what you may need your credit for in the near future.
- Closing out or canceling old cards and credit lines — This drops your average age of accounts which is necessary for building great credit.
- Paying cash for everything — As crazy as this sounds, being able to budget and pay things off in full can in fact hurt you because it doesn't go on your credit. By doing this you have no credit which is essentially just as bad as having a poor credit score because lenders have nothing to go off of in order to determine your ability to pay things on time; lenders want to see people who have handled debt responsibly.

Monitor Your Credit

Applications like myFICO, Credit Karma, the Turbo app, and Experian app make it easier to monitor your credit. While apps like Credit Karma do not give you your actual fico scores, (meaning they could be higher or lower than your actual score), what makes their vantage scores useful is that you are able to actively see what components impact your credit. Being able to see what positively and negatively affects your credit allows you to better play the game and tweak your score to what you want.

The Experian app offers what's called "Experian Boost". There are several things that you pay monthly that only report negative activity to the bureaus but not the positive (power bill, cable bill, etc.). What this allows you to do is self-report this activity and get extra points on your credit for positive payment history. This method can be useful, however the second you remove it, your score will fall. So think it through before just jumping into it.

If you have been renting for a while, there are companies out there that will report this payment history to your credit. Some people have years of positive history that they aren't utilizing to raise their scores.

Certain credit cards offer Fico score monitoring just for carrying the card. The credit bureaus (Experian, Equifax, Transunion) are required by law to give you access to your credit report free of charge once every calendar year. You can do this by going to www.AnnualCreditReport.com. However, be aware they charge for the actual scores.

Hard Pull Vs Soft Pull

- A hard inquiry, also known as a hard pull, occurs when a financial institution (credit card issuer, lender, etc.) checks your credit to determine your creditworthiness and make a lending decision.

- A soft inquiry, also known as a soft pull, occurs when you personally check your credit, or when a financial institution (credit card issuer, lender, etc.) checks your credit to pre-approve you for offers. This type of "pull" doesn't affect your score nor does it show up.

Quick Tip: One way to check to see if you are pre-approved for certain credit cards or if you will be targeted for certain credit offers is to visit CreditCards.com and use their Card Match tool. This tool does a soft pull on your credit, so it won't show up or impact your credit at all, but you will be able to see where you stand before going after a credit card. Also, the free apps that allow you to check your credit (Credit Karma, Credit Sesame, etc.) will show you various cards that may help improve your credit as well as those that you have good odds of being approved for. Be mindful that the cards they show are from their affiliates.

Credit Repair

The tools are out there for you to do this yourself, but if you don't mind spending the money, have a reputable company remove old or paid off accounts, update info, and correct inaccuracies. This will quickly increase your score. One of the best ways to improve your credit is to simply pay your bills, plain and simple.

Be advised, some of the accounts on your credit although they are negatively reporting, they are a part of the calculation for average age of accounts, so once you pay them in full, the debt is gone but your credit could potentially take a small dip because that history is gone as well. Eliminating bad debt is always the right choice though.

Good Debt Vs Bad Debt

Too much debt of any kind is bad so avoid this at all costs!

Some examples of "good debt" would be debt that carries a low interest rate (thus costing you as little money as possible), and generates money for you. For example, a loan used to obtain a property that will generate monthly revenue or used to start a business that will increase your income and net worth is good debt.

Debt you can control, such as a credit card (if used properly) is considered good debt. Reason being, if you pay with a credit card correctly, you eliminate the interest all together and essentially get a line of credit in your pocket to use for free each month (O.P.M in action). Conversely, if you are going to let the interest accrue, then the same credit card becomes bad debt due to the high interest rate. The point is to use as much of "Other People's Money" as you can with little to no interest, so you profit from free money. This is a key determining factor of what can make debt "good"

Essentially, bad debt is when you borrow money to purchase something that does not generate income, add to your net worth, will cost you more in interest than the value gained from the transaction, or depreciates instead of going up in value.

> **Quick Tip:** A boat or an exotic car could be considered both bad debt and a liability because it does not add value, it depreciates and constantly costs you money. However, some bad debt and liabilities can be turned into good debt assets. For example, if I took that same boat and rented it out for fishing trips or parties and events (depending on the boat type) it now pays for itself and generates income for me. As well, if I had a Rolls Royce and rented it out for music videos, weddings, and other events it pays for itself and becomes a new income stream.

Credit Self-Assessment

Take this time to identify your current situation. As you answer the following questions be honest, be detailed and even make itemized charts to organize your answers. This information will help you determine where you are currently and help you determine the steps needed to get where you want to be.

- If you are new to credit, what steps will you take to start off positively?
- What steps will you take to ensure your credit stays positive?
- Is becoming an authorized user an option for you?
- What are your current credit scores for the three bureaus?
- Do you have your actual FICO scores?
- What scores would you like to have?
- Do you have a copy of your current year credit reports?
- How many positive/negative accounts do you have?
- Any serious delinquencies or derogatory marks? How many?
- How many closed accounts do you have? Any reporting negatively?
- How many inquiries do you currently have and when do they fall off?
- What types of credit do you have on your report?
- Is your credit report accurate?
- Do you utilize any credit apps?
- Do you take advantage of printing your credit report free once annually?

- What are the top factors negatively affecting your credit right now?
- What are the top factors positively affecting your credit right now?
- If your credit is less than perfect, what mistakes can you avoid in the future?
- What steps are you taking, or will you take to improve your credit?
- How often do you monitor your credit?

Investments

What Should You Invest In?

I want to focus on one of the biggest investments the wealthy and financially stable make that others do not. This one investment can be the difference between obtaining financial freedom or remaining poor. Before I get into what this investment is, let me explain a few things.

Whenever you hear about creating passive income, residual income or any other term that has been coined today to express having money come in that you do little to no work for it to continue flowing in, the first thing you hear them say is you need to invest but they never tell you what to invest in.

When it comes to investing, not all investments are created equally. What many fail to tell you is that certain investments are only available to you if you meet certain requirements like net worth restrictions, on hand cash requirements, liquidity requirements, and how much you can invest immediately, etc. These factors are what separates many of the investments they tell you about from the ones that are available to you at your current financial state. With this in mind, understand a lot of things are not even available to you until your financial foundation has been set. It's all a process and takes time, so the quicker you get started the better.

Me, Myself, & I

As simple as this may seem, the biggest investment that financially free individuals make that poor people (poor credit, poor financial health, etc.) do not is in themselves. **YOU** are the first long term investment that you must make to not only reach your financial goals, but also maintain them once you get there. I discussed how the education system doesn't teach any form of financial basics (credit, finances, taxes, etc.), and do harm to students by not preparing them for financial freedom, but to become part of the rat race chasing a check every week, exchanging their time for minimal wages, and ensuring they do not understand the basics of finances so they make bad decisions and end up in debt which puts money in the pockets of others while they remain poor.

At this point you're probably thinking why so many people say go to school and get a good job. This is because they only understand things on the surface, but were never taught to dig deeper into what truly gives you financial freedom, so your money works for you instead of you killing yourself working for money.

Wealthy people often say get educated and never stop learning. This seems to contradict their views on the school system, however when they say this, they actually mean that you need to seek additional education outside of the confines of traditional education. You need to get educated on how the world around you works, understand how the money you make works, understand the banking institutions around you, and so on. Before successful people reached their goals, they had to invest in themselves to build the proper foundation then continue educating themselves to increase or maintain what they built.

Wealth is a byproduct of increased financial literacy and understanding of the world around you. Financial literacy and increased understanding are in no way a byproduct of wealth. Stop thinking that if you get more money, you will magically know how to manage it and how it works.

At one time it was reported that within two years of retirement, 78% of NFL (National Football League) players were either bankrupt or under some financial duress. It was reported that within five years of retirement, 60% of NBA (National Basketball Association) players were bankrupt. Additionally, a large percent of lottery winners end up broke, or file bankruptcy within three to five years of winning.

This, and many other statistics, prove that simply giving you a lump sum of money would do you more harm than good if you lack the financial literacy to grow it or maintain it properly. Therefore, investing in yourself is the one of the biggest investments needed if you want financial freedom.

Investing in You

We live in a digital age, and I tell people all the time the internet is for more than just social media and finding funny memes. You have a plethora of information on an assortment of topics at your fingertips all you have to do is access it. Reading is essential to financial freedom because it shifts your perceptions and elevates your mind to new possibilities you may not have even thought about. What you put into your mind is what you will get out of it, so if you want financial freedom then educate yourself daily on how the game of life, the game of credit, the game of finances operates.

I spoke in depth on budgeting which allows you to take control of your finances. As well, this is helping you invest in yourself because you gain the discipline to control your money, you eliminate bad habits and gain good ones, you are training yourself to monitor the flow of your money and make necessary adjustments to get the intended results. Again, this seems small, but you are pouring a solid foundation in order to handle more money and responsibility down the road.

Saving money with a purpose allows you to invest in your future plans which will help increase your patience and better deal with delayed gratification. In many areas, think of a crock-pot not a microwave.

If you struggle with handling tasks on your own, then seek out a mentor or someone who has already overcome what you are facing, or they are currently where you want to be. Everyone always stresses the importance of networking when it comes to a job, but it is just as important to network in order to gain knowledge.

Stop getting a job just for the paycheck and understand many of you are paid by multi-million/multi-billion-dollar corporations that train you on how they function and allow you to see the day to day operations. Having a job that fits your dream career or the business you want to open in the future allows you to get first hand training on exactly what to do to be successful.

Also, you can't be afraid of responsibility the higher up the chain you move gets you experience in running a business. Depending on your position you will gain valuable experience in how the finances work, hiring firing process, what goes into training an employee, associated business costs and so on. As well this will give you the opportunity to network with vendors and other key players so that you have a standing relationship built when you are ready to do something on your own. Don't work just for the money, work for the knowledge, the experience, the connections and continued education you get on how the world around you operates.

As you continue to be educated daily and learn new concepts, make sure you develop your listening skills. Growing up my dad would always say "you have two ears and one mouth which means you should be listening twice as much as you talk". You would be amazed at how much you can learn from someone just by listening and letting them do all the talking. From my own experience, even if someone starts to tell you something you already know, let them finish because chances are, they will tell you a few added things that you did not know. In addition, people like those that are teachable so no matter how high or far you go, never stop learning. It's always something out there you did not know.

Understand you can't do it all on your own and as you grow you will start to build a team (accountant, attorney, employees...etc.). You do not have to wait until you reach the final level in order to start working on this team because established relationships are a valuable investment. Get out and talk to people and see who meshes well with your future goals. Similar to when I discussed financial institutions it is important to ensure you are building a foundation for now but never lose sight of building for where you want to end up. Ensure your team fits what's to come more so than what is currently.

If you do not plan to establish your own business, you can still establish a team for when you move into various levels of management. When I say management, understand I am referring to a position of overseeing a group of individuals to carry out a common goal. Principals, boat captains, and real estate brokers all have a position where they manage. As you climb the ladder of success you can start to assemble your team and establish the right relationships to ensure your current and future success.

> **Quick Tip #1:** None of this is overnight it is all a process, most investments are, but if you plan to do anything of substance in the future investing in yourself is crucial.

Do not be afraid of change or concepts that challenge your current way of thinking. We stress what to learn but it is often just as important to unlearn. To be blunt, many of us were taught about life, money, and personal finance from people that did not fully grasp the concepts themselves so instead of generational wealth and stability it led to generational mediocrity where everyone was trying to find their way in the game of life. This is nothing to be ashamed of or feel bad about because in today's society there are many instances where the children end up learning more than their parents then go back to teach them. In my life I have educated my parents on everything from real estate, taxes and the benefits their corporations held…etc. I say this because while investing in yourself you will come across notions that go against your core ideals. As you invest in yourself change is great and you have to be open to principles that do not sound or look like what you were taught. You can't follow the same paths and expect a different result; to get what you have never had you must do things you have never done.

> **Quick Tip #2:** No one ever got wealthy or free staying in their comfort zone. If you want something, if you want to expand your territory, you are going to have to go out and make it happen. As you invest in yourself you are your biggest obstacle. You will have to adjust your habits, your ways, your thinking and overall outlook on the world around you; the battle and initial investment starts in your mind.

Understand when you hear the word millionaire it's a mindset first followed by actions that materialize and manifest those things that are not. What you say is just as important as what you think. Statements like "I can't" and "I don't know how" shut the brain down and prevent it from strategically working out the current issue. This is why affirmations are so important when you speak about yourself, and current situation. You truly shape your atmosphere by the way you think and speak. You have to get out of your own way and allow the process to work. If you think "how can I" this allows you to work it out, then when you speak it to be already done it gives you the confidence to make it happen. Do not think or speak yourself into nothingness.

Investing in You

The power of "no" was covered in a previous section because it is important to not give away all that you have obtained. On the journey of investing in yourself do not be afraid of giving a no, likewise don't be afraid of receiving a no or failing. So many people focus on what if they fail or receive a no that they do not prepare for success or being told yes. Instead of allowing your no's and failures to become weights that hold you down you have to shift your paradigm and use them as stepping stones to get where you want to be. ***Do not view failures as negatives because in essence you did not fail but you figured out ways to achieve other outcomes and you learned what not to do in the future.***

Successful people understand the value of failure and a no; yes, I said value. When you fail, or don't reach your expected result, you now have something you can assess and better plan for future attempts. When met with failure or a no, many people just give up or get discouraged. While investing in yourself remember you are working to combat your thoughts and words so stay positive and continue fighting for what you want.

We all have the same twenty-four hours in a day, what are you doing with yours? In the same manner it is important to budget your money it is important to properly manage your time. Time is a valuable asset so use it wisely and don't let anyone waste it by any means. As you budget you will see areas where you are wasting money; in the same manner as you properly manage your time you will see that you wasted hours binge watching that tv series when you could've been making progress in your life. If any of this makes you cringe, makes you feel uneasy or makes you think "that's asking too much" then it is time to self-assess and invest in your discipline and control of "self". It seems small but just think of the amount of discipline it takes to work long hours sometimes in a business you own and do not have to come in if you don't want to. Think about how much discipline it takes to have several accounts of money and credit cards with high limits and only spend that which is necessary and not go overboard with wants.

> **Quick Tip:** By now you are probably thinking "this is just too much work and too much effort in order to get the life I want". You are probably second guessing if you even want to do all that it takes, and if not, that's ok you can easily remain in your current state and be content. The world is full of people who want everything with the least amount of work. Today's society wants an abundant harvest of crops without plowing the ground. If you feel yourself wanting to be lazy when it comes to your own well-being and financial freedom you have to then determine how important you are…to you (sounds crazy but think about that for a second).

As you invest in yourself in order to positively progress it is important to monitor the company you keep. As we discussed budgets, I stressed the importance of either being able to control yourself around people that aren't headed where you are. If they have poor spending habits, you need to stick to your plan and if you are easily influenced then you may want to create a bit of distance. Similarly, if you are surrounded by lazy people who are not trying to become financially free, move up the latter or open a successful business then you have to do what's best for you. If you are trying to soak up knowledge and develop lasting relationships at work, then associating yourself with those that are always late and produce sub-par work is not the best plan of action. Furthermore, if you are trying to establish a successful, perpetual business then having dealings with people that have a reputation of stealing, poor customer service, failed businesses, and poor financial literacy then you are destined to not succeed. Who you keep around you can positively or negatively influence you, but it can also influence the way others view you. In many instances those that started out with you will not be those that make it with you to the end and that's ok because growth is necessary to reach certain levels.

Protect your peace, exercise, eat right, pray, meditate, speak your affirmations daily, keep positive open-minded thinking; no matter what you choose it is important to stay healthy physically, emotionally and spiritually. There is no point in building a great life, obtaining financial freedom, having great credit, amassing wealth, establishing a successful career or building a great business if you are not around to enjoy it or healthy enough to enjoy the benefits. It is ok to eat your favorite meals or have that glass of wine but remember life is all about balance and moderation. You want to ensure that you are happy and healthy, including your mental health, as you build in life because the term wealth does not just refer to money but also the state of your well-being.

In my early years my dad constantly said, "dress for success" or "always dress like you're going somewhere". He did not mean to the store or to the playground, but in life. This is not to say that you should get caught up on labels and blow money on expensive clothes. But as you invest in yourself make sure you invest in the way you look and carry yourself because someone is always watching. I once showed up to a simple interview in a suit and tie; I got the job without an interview because the manager liked the way I carried myself before ever knowing anything about me. Life is chess not checkers so always be mindful of where you want to go as well as where you are currently. Your knowledge, the way you carry yourself and the way you dress should speak volumes about you and people shouldn't be able to tell if you are an employee or the owner.

Investment Self-Assessment

Take this time to identify your current situation. As you answer the following questions be honest, be detailed and even make itemized charts to organize your answers. This information will help you determine where you are currently and help you determine the steps needed to get where you want to be.

- What is the highest level of school you have completed? Why?
- What is the highest level of school that you would like to complete? Why?
- Do you have a relationship with key figures at your educational institution?
- Who are they? How does it benefit you (teachers, professors, deans… etc.)?
- Do you invest in yourself? In what ways?
- How often do you educate yourself outside of a school setting?
- What forms of outside education do you utilize (books, seminars… etc.)?
- What are the last 5 books you read and what were they about?
- Are you using your time wisely?
- Have you discovered areas where you could better utilize that time?
- Outside of social media do you utilize the internet to invest in yourself?
- Do you have a mentor or someone that is currently where you want to be?

- Besides a paycheck, what benefits do you get from your current job?
- Do you have a relationship with those in upper management?
- How often do you network and build positive relationships?
- How well do you take hearing no? How do you take failure?
- What type of company do you keep? Will these people hinder or help you?
- What steps are you taking to get out of your comfort zone?

Basics of Buying a Car

Lenders & Dealerships Always Want Something

- You will need a valid driver license
- Proof of current insurance
- Check stubs to prove income
- How you plan to pay for the car (cash, personal check, financing…etc.)
- Your credit score and history (this is important because not only does it show that you can be trusted to pay on time, and in full, depending on the price of the car you want lenders would like to see that you have previously handled certain car levels. If you want a $70k vehicle they would at least like to see that you have handled an account in that range or above)
- Depending on your credit they may want references or a co-signer
- Depending on the price of the vehicle they may ask for bank statements so they can assess your cash flow and/or confirm funds for a cash purchase or down payment
- If you are trading in a car then you will need the current title for the car, current vehicle registration, possibly service records and a car free of all your personal belongings. Also, if you still have a balance

on your trade-in then you will need the necessary documentation so they can see what the pay-off is on the vehicle.

- When purchasing a car out of state it is important to pay attention to how that state handles this because you may be facing additional fees, taxes, transport costs and paperwork; although in some cases you may just find the car you want cheaper in another state.

Do This...Don't Do That

- When you enter a dealership, understand they have the upper hand because you are walking into their territory. Most people increase this simply by giving too much personal information up front.
- Even if you are desperate for a car, never let the salesperson know this; negotiating is like poker, never show your hand before time or give away signs of your true position be it negative or positive.
- Going to the dealership should be your time to test drive vehicles and really see what you want so that you can make a plan in order to get the vehicle for the best deal.
- When choosing a car try to pick one that the dealer has on the lot (or in stock) if you choose a special color and the dealer has to special order it or go out of their way to get the vehicle for you chances are they are not going to be so quick to negotiate with you or give you a better deal.
- If you do plan to negotiate the price (every situation is different) then start with a price lower than what you're willing to pay because it's in fact going to go up. A trick that has worked is to put the responsibility of the spending limit on someone not present. For example, if you offer $28k and the dealer counters with $33k then you could tell them that your best and final is $31k and your (wife/husband/girlfriend...whomever) is not going to let you go any higher (you could also mention "another lot" was willing to do better). At this point

the salesperson has a third party they can't argue with and in many cases will do their best to close the deal. Truth is you want to buy, they want to sell. The only thing in the middle is the price and terms.

- Walking away during negotiating is not a sign of weakness but one of power because it says to the salesperson you aren't desperate. If your terms are denied simply tell them, you appreciate their efforts and sorry things couldn't work out but if anything changes, they have your number. In some cases, this will lead to a call back and better terms being offered.

- Similar to how you would put lenders against one another in order to gain the upper hand the same can be true here. Once you find the vehicle you want, and you see a price the dealership has it at you want to email or call various dealerships and ask them to price out the car you want to buy (out the door price). By doing this you will most likely get a range of prices for the exact same car giving you the necessary tools to get the best deal because the salesperson now knows they could lose you if they don't play ball. Additionally, just like with the loan example you can use this information to work the dealerships against one another, so they essentially fight to get the sale giving you the best deal.

- When getting financing for a car understand that the dealership doesn't care about you or your credit, so they are going to shop around your credit. Understand they are NOT looking for the best deal for you but for the one that pads their pockets the most. Another way to control the interest rate and the amount of times your credit is pulled is to get pre-approved from your own bank prior to car shopping (you will know how much car you can afford and will generally get better terms from a bank you already have a relationship with). By doing this it's harder for a dealership to play around because they know the bank will assess the vehicle based on what it's actually worth minus all the padded fees and add-ons you don't need anyway. As well, this takes some of the control the dealership has away.

Quick Tip: When discussing the vehicle if you plan to pay cash or already have a check in hand from your bank do not say this up front and do not sign or agree to any credit applications because your focus is getting the price and terms you want before showing your hand. If you tell this too early in the negotiations most finance managers will refuse to give you any type of deal because you are essentially taking away another way they make money.

- We previously discussed that when properly using a credit card you should aim to never pay interest. The same applies here the more interest you pay the more the bank wins. If you can pay cash for a car do so, although you won't get any credit history for. If you do finance a vehicle, aim to pay it off as quickly as possible so you limit how much "extra" you are paying for this depreciating liability.

Do This...Don't Do That

- When it comes to trade-ins know exactly what it's worth so that you are robbed of money you could've gotten. If you choose to sell the car on your own chances are you may get more money than initially anticipated. Understand while you can do everything under one roof with the dealer (buy a car, get financing and trade your car) the more you do under that one roof the more power you give the dealership.
- The job of the salesperson is to sell. They don't care about your situation or anything going on with you. Understand anytime a salesperson is speaking to you their job is to convince you as quickly as possible to close the deal and take advantage of everything you do not know. I won't say they lie but if you do not know that certain fees do not have to be added they sure aren't going to tell you.
- Salespeople typically use scare tactics and dialogue that pressures you into add-ons you may not even need. Unless that extended warranty is negotiated into the price of the vehicle (without raising it of course), or if that expensive dent protection doesn't just come with the car then you need to determine the true value to you personally

that each one has. If the cost added outweighs the value to you then don't get it. (car salespeople want to close now, now, now and plan to do so by any means; do the deal on your terms and on your timing not theirs).

- Extended warranties sound nice on the surface but understand that when you get one of these they come with several downsides. In reality an extended warranty can boil down to just being a souped-up service contract. This warranty ensures that you get all your services done at a particular dealership and because of that the prices that they charge are locked in for you. When every single rule is followed a warranty can come in handy, conversely a dealership can deny your claims on minute technicalities if they see fit. If there is a clause that stipulates you must meet all service dates and you miss one or are late by a few days, they can use this as leverage to justify why they don't want to accept your claim. Do your homework, ensure it works for you and that you are getting the most value possible.

- When talking to a salesperson normal conversational dialogue and dynamics do not apply here. I'm in no way saying be rude and nasty but understand with your money on the line you have the right to remain firm when you say things and it is up to you on what you choose to answer. As previously stated, the more information you give up typically the more it will be used against you so the dealership can maintain the upper hand.

- The more information you divulge then the more information the salesperson knows what tactics to use in order to give a pitch that is tailored to your situation. It is smart in these situations to sometimes answer a question with a question. If you are asked how much the car would have to be priced at to get you to buy, instead of giving an actual figure, respond by telling them they are the expert and what is the lowest offer they are willing to accept. Remember the salesperson is only human and in the same manner they try to gain information from you, this is your chance to turn the tables. (The more questions you ask the more information you can gather and place that pressure back on the salesperson).

- Watch out for the dealer delivery fee because in many cases this is a ridiculous amount of money that they have you pay because the car was dropped off to them and they put gas in it (yes you can request a full tank of gas on a car you purchase). They are essentially trying to make you pay for a service that implies they bring the car to you when in reality you have to come and pick up your own car. Try your best to negotiate this as low as you can.

- Truth is you do not need paint protection, rust protection, rust proofing, or fabric protection. If you regularly detail your car it will stay clean, a good wax every six months will keep the paint looking new (now there are all sorts of ceramic protectants on the market), and the way the steel in cars is coated it comes with help to prevent rust anyway. Bottom line, say no!

- Cars today come with several accessories; these accessories come with a nice price tag as well. In many cases you can find these accessories somewhere else for a lower price. If you have done your homework and found them elsewhere cheaper, you can either purchase them on your own or ask that the dealer match the prices. (Keep in mind you want to cut your costs and keep debts low or non-existent. By letting the dealer add the accessories, even if they price match, that price is rolled into the deal. That amount of money is financed, which means the interest you pay over the life of the loan will cause you to pay more for those accessories in the long run anyway. In this case paying cash for it eliminates all of that. Get only the accessories you need. Don't waste money on something just because you think it's cool.

- Have your own insurance because in most cases dealer "in-house" insurance is not a good value to you. These white label products (insurance products with standard terms and conditions from an insurance company with the dealer name stamped on it basically) are generally overpriced because every party involved (insurance company, car dealer and car maker) all have their hands in the pot, and you are left with the bill. With your own insurance you can generally get a better deal for the same, if not better, coverage.

Why is Any of That Important?

Dealerships often use what's called the 4-square method (no not that fun game many of us played in elementary school). With this it's generally a piece of paper that has four boxes labeled trade-in value, price (of the vehicle you want to get), down payment and monthly payment. This system is used because it's easier to confuse a buyer and easy to manipulate numbers in order to sell the illusion of a good deal. The salesperson hopes you will focus on only one box, (primarily the monthly payment box) that way they can shift numbers and continue selling the deal.

By doing your own research and by coming prepared you break up this trick and you take control of each box individually. As we continue to discuss, you want to take, and maintain, as much power as you possibly can from the dealership. If you already have set in stone figures you are bringing to the table, they have less smoke and mirrors to use when persuading you (research, research, and more research! Trust me the dealer has done theirs and has made a ton selling dreams to unsuspecting buyers).

> **Quick Tip:** Many of the guidelines for buying a home can work here too. Do your research and negotiate; they can only say no. Focus on the value you get out of the deal, the better your credit the better your terms. Lastly, maintain control by shopping around and know costs and valuations up front.

When to Buy?

There is no magical time to buy. Plain and simple we can only take what has happened previously and mix it with the "crunch times" for dealerships and analyze the common sense of supply and demand to determine when to buy.

Supply and demand will always stand true! If there is a popular new car out chances, are you will not be able to get the discounts you want because the dealer has a plethora of people lined up to buy the car so there is no need to negotiate with you. So, waiting until the vehicle is not trending so much would be the best strategy here.

Dealerships typically have yearly, quarterly, and monthly quotas that have to be met. This means if you choose to purchase a car between October to November, or at the end of the month, or at the end of any of these quota deadlines your odds of getting the terms you want increase.

Going to the dealership at the end of the day can sometimes be useful because if it has been a slow day some salespeople may be desperate for a sale; as well coming at the end of the day doesn't leave much time and they do not want a potential sale to walk out of the door, so they may be more lenient in working the deal in order to get it done.

> **Quick Tip:** With the car market the way it is today many dealerships have taken advantage of chip shortages and other part shortages. As a result, they have marked up the price of some vehicles by as much as $70k over MSRP. This means many consumers are substantially overpaying for vehicles and are ending up with a vehicle that is not worth even close to what they paid. As I have stated before, research, research, and research some more before getting trapped in a terrible deal.

Bad Credit? No Credit? No Problem...Wrong!!

As you may have noticed by now having good credit is important in the major decisions you want to make. This is the worst statement that a person could ever make; but because the dealerships and lenders care more about their profits than you positively building your credit portfolio, they will say anything it takes to get you in the door and get the deal done. Is it possible to get approved on these lots with bad credit? Yes, it is; what they don't tell you is that with bad credit this deal will come with extortionately high interest, high monthly payments, terrible terms (60, 72…etc. basically how long or short the loan will be financed out), and in many cases a high down payment.

> **Quick Tip:** If your credit profile is established it is possible for the bank to fully finance your vehicle eliminating the need for a down payment.

To Buy or to Lease, That is the Question...

This decision is situation specific. The amount of value you get from each is what should determine which you decide on. I won't spend too much time on this area but be aware of the possible fees and taxes that come with a lease (because this is situation specific you will have to do your homework on which best suits your needs and financial situation).

When buying a car, we have already discussed items like the purchase price, possible down payment, the interest on the loan, terms, monthly payments and a possible sale/trade-in price of that car in the end.

With a lease you have a down payment but instead of a traditional car note you have a monthly payment while the bank lets you use the car. The terms here indicate how long you will keep the car which can range from two to five years given the situation. During this time you are only allowed to drive a set number of miles per year, typically between 12,000 and 15,000 miles. The miles per year can be increased but it will also increase the monthly payment. For example, if your lease agreement is for three years and 12,000 miles per year when your lease is up, your mileage is expected to be at or less than 36,000 miles. If you have 36,427 miles the dealer does have the right to charge you for the additional 427 miles because it is over the agreed mileage.

> **Quick Tip #1:** Do your research because some dealers won't tell you that they offer such programs as mileage forgiveness and mileage rollover. In short, they will forgive you for going over the allotted mileage (up to a certain amount) or they will roll over any unused mileage into your next lease.
>
> **Quick Tip #2:** In a lease agreement they expect to get the car back in great condition. If the car has anything they deem to be "excessive wear and tear" then you will be charged for it.

By now I know you are probably thinking why would anyone ever lease a car? The answer is that with this method it can be cheaper to obtain the car you want, you can get a new car every couple of years, and in some cases the value can be greater to you. If you wanted a Rolls Royce of course this is going to cost you a lot. With a lease you don't tie up all that extra money that you could be doing something else with in a depreciating object.

Quick Tip #3: Going after a vehicle that is fresh off lease can allow you to get a well maintained, low mileage vehicle you have always wanted without the price tag. The vehicle must be sold at a depreciated value even though most of the lease it probably sat in a garage.

Car Buying Self-Assessment

Take this time to identify your current situation. As you answer the following questions be honest, be detailed and even make itemized charts to organize your answers. This information will help you determine where you are currently and help you determine the steps needed to get where you want to be.

- Do you need a new car or want a new car? Why?
- Have you determined if getting a car fits into your budget at this time?
- Is your credit strong enough to get approved for a car?
- Do you have all the necessary items to start the process?
- Do you have a financial institution willing to finance the vehicle?
- What car do you want and what benefits does it offer?
- How long does this type of car typically last with regular maintenance?
- How much is the yearly regular maintenance on your car of choice?
- How many miles are on the car?
- What is the overall condition of the car inside and out?
- Has it been wrecked or sustained water damage of some sort?
- Is there an accurate Carfax on the vehicle?
- Will you be making a trade in? How much is it worth?
- Do you have a buyer or are you willing to take what the dealer offers?

- Will you need a down payment? How much and do you currently have it?
- Will you set up automatic payments on this car or handle it yourself?
- Is the car still under a manufacturer's warranty?
- What specifically does your warranty cover exactly?
- Do you have an established relationship with a particular dealer?
- Have you checked for online specials the dealer may be running?
- Is the car you want currently in stock at the dealer you chose?
- Did you shop around for the best possible price from a dealer?
- Did you check the terms/rates of multiple financial institutions?

Basics of Buying a Home

Types of Home Loans

The following information can vary depending on the lender and your personal factors such as credit score, down payment, and price of the home.

- ***Conventional/Fixed Rate Mortgages*** are available in 10/15/20/30/40 year terms; 15 and 30 are the most common. This loan type is safe because you know your payment up front and it won't change over time. This loan type can be conforming or non-conforming; this simply means the loan conforms and fits within the limits set by Fannie Mae and Freddie Mac or they are non-conforming and fall within the parameters of a jumbo loan.

- ***Interest Only Mortgages*** give you the option to pay only the interest portion of the monthly payment instead of the entire amount during the first 5-10 years. This isn't ideal because it slows down the repayment process, but if you need the extra help, it can be useful. After the interest only period the loan is paid in full like a conventional loan

- ***Adjustable-Rate Mortgages (ARM)*** come in many forms but the basic premise is that the interest rate changes over the life of the loan. The rate changes as the economy and cost of borrowing money fluctuates. The rate stays the same during the first 5 years and is free to change during the remaining 25 years.

- ***FHA Loans*** are guaranteed by the Federal Housing Administration, so they come with built in mortgage insurance to protect against you not being able to repay the loan. The down payment on these loans is generally smaller with this loan type.

- ***VA Loans*** are designed to make it easier for veterans, and sometimes spouses, to buy a home. They don't require a downpayment and are backed by the Department of Veteran Affairs

- ***USDA Loans*** target moderate to low-income borrowers who want to buy a home in a rural area. There are income restrictions, and the home must be purchased in a USDA eligible area. This loan type does not require a down payment in most cases.

- ***Combo/Piggyback Loans*** are special loans that come about when your down payment is less than 20% and you combine two loan types to avoid paying private mortgage insurance.

- ***Balloon Mortgages*** allow you to pay interest only for a certain amount of time then require the full principal amount after the initial period ends.

- ***Jumbo Loans*** are for loans that are too big for a traditional loan that the federal government can purchase or guarantee. With this loan type the down payment is larger and some of the interest rates aren't as low as smaller loan types.

Some Pros & Cons

With a conventional mortgage they can be used for your primary residence, second home or investment property. Overall borrowing costs tend to be lower than other mortgage types even if the interest rate is higher. Once you have gained your 20% equity you can ask the lender to cancel your PMI (private mortgage insurance). In some cases, you can put down as little as 3% and the minimum FICO score required is 620 or higher. Lenders typically look for a 45 to 50% debt to income ratio and require significant documentation to verify income, assets, down payment and employment.

FHA loans can be helpful when you do not have a large down payment saved up and your credit may not be the best. A 500-credit score with at least 10% down could be enough to get you into the home you want. The standard is a 580-credit score with 3.5% down (this is the FHA minimum). Depending on how much you put down FHA requires a mortgage insurance premium be paid up front and one to be paid annually during the life of the loan (this can increase the overall cost of your mortgage).

VA Loans are low interest, do not require a down payment or PMI, the closing costs generally have a cap and may be paid by the seller. There is a fee charge as a percentage to offset the program's cost to taxpayers. This fee can be rolled into most VA loans or paid upfront.

Fixed Rate mortgages generally require more interest with a longer term, it takes longer to build equity in your home and the interest rates are typically higher than ARM's.

With Adjustable-Rate Mortgages because they fluctuate your mortgage payments could become unaffordable causing you to default on your loan and ruin your credit. If the home value decreased this would make it substantially harder to refinance or sell your home until the loan resets with a better rate.

Jumbo loans require more money down, typically a 700 FICO score or higher is required although some lender may consider a 660. Your debt-to-income ratio can't exceed 45% and you must have significant assets in cash or savings account generally totaling 10% of the loan amount.

Credit

- Your credit file basically shows the bank how likely you are to repay money that is lent to you.
- With a credit score above 740 the bank will typically give you the best interest possible.
- With a credit score above 760 the banks will, to an extent, throw money at you because you are more likely to repay a loan without any problems. Additionally, they may offer you lender credits, rebates, and other money saving perks.

Debts and High Interest Debts

Prior to buying a home you want to really focus on eliminating as much, if not all, high interest debt you may currently have. This includes loans, credit cards, personal loans, or anything else bearing high interest. Having this type of debt lingering will limit the type of loans you can get (it affects your debt-to-income ratio).

> Quick Tip: While student loan debt can affect the calculations, a lender uses when buying a home if it is 4% interest or lower you may be able to get by with the payment strategy you already have in place. If it's 5% and above, you may want to go ahead and accelerate your payment plan because while over time it can help your average age of accounts it will cost you more to pay it long term than to pay it off early; you keep more money and gain higher value from early prepayment in this situation.

How Much Down?

This depends on what loan type you go with and what your credit file looks like. This amount could vary from 3.5% to 10 or 20%

Get Pre-Qualified

This is the process where you go speak with a lender (hopefully before looking at home or anything else) to see where you currently stand and how much home you can afford.

As a licensed real estate agent, I can say no one likes their time to be wasted. Getting prequalified saves you and the agent time because it keeps the agent from showing you properties outside of your budget and it keeps you from falling in love with the "perfect house" only to discover you can't afford it.

A great benefit of getting prequalified is that you already have everything you need waiting with your lender so in the event you do find that perfect home you can go ahead and put in an offer the same day and possibly get the property before someone else does. If you like the home, it's a great chance someone else does too and prequalification can give you a possible leg up.

What Do You Want?

When looking for a home sit down and write out what you want (be realistic) and then make a list with your deal breakers. Deal breakers are not things that could easily be fixed like paint color or kitchen cabinets, but things like are you fine with a long commute, is the home by a busy street or interstate and you're a light sleeper, you require a larger yard, and the home has no yard at all…etc. What you WANT in your home is not always what you NEED doing this will help you better narrow down the homes.

What Do Lenders Want?

- One to two years of previous tax returns to show proof of income
- Your full credit reports and scores to see how you "pay your bills"
- Two to six months (but could be up to two years) worth of bank statements to see how you manage your money, average daily balances, cash flow consistency, proof of income and expenses
- Check stubs to prove income and show fluctuations
- Some lenders like to see that you currently have two to six months of your expenses saved up
- Some lenders like to see proof of other sources of income, accounts, properties you own, assets and liabilities you may have, and anything else that is a part of your portfolio that could help or hinder your ability to repay the loan.

> **Quick Tip:** Banks like to see things they can "take" in the event you don't pay them their money back, plain and simple. In addition, if you are claiming to be self-employed the bank analyzes you harder

and makes you jump through more hoops (providing proof and documentation) in order to get approved

Do I Need an Agent?

As a licensed agent I will try to be as unbiased as possible when answering this question.

When a seller enters a listing agreement they are obligated to pay, let's say, a 5% commission. This commission is split 2.5% to the listing agent who represents the seller and 2.5% to the selling agent (or sometimes referred to as the buyer's agent) who represents the buyers.

Generally, this 5% commission is paid regardless if you choose to utilize your own agent or not when purchasing a property. So, because the commission is being paid anyway, why not have a professional help you through a process they've facilitated and been in more than you have.

If this is your first or second time buying a property, having a professional to guide you through can help you out tremendously. A good agent can save you money by properly negotiating the deal while a bad agent could cost you more than you should've put out.

When to Buy?

The average buyer believes the best time to buy is between spring and summer, while winter is considered to be the worst time to buy. Some sellers follow this same notion and as a result more inventory tends to be on the market. This sounds like the ideal situation for a picky buyer looking for the perfect home, but this type of group thinking can lead to increased competition. In real estate more competition can lead to a bidding war and drive up the price of the desired property.

Although during the winter months there tends to be less inventory the sellers that list during this time are typically more "motivated" which could result in you getting a better deal on your home.

The real estate market crash of 2008 has some buyers waiting for it to happen again so they can get that perfect home for little to no money from a desperate seller. This is not a good idea because there is no solid way to determine when or if this will ever happen again. If you are the type who is looking for a home and wants to protect yourself from an unseen crash, think of this. If you plan to live there less than four years you are better off renting if you are fearful of the unknown but if you plan to stay in the property long term and do not plan on selling it, then it won't matter anyway.

> **Quick Tip:** There is no "best time to buy" but rather a time for better deals and value you get when purchasing a home due to less competition in the market and motivated sellers. However, with the current state of the market the best time to buy would be when you are prepared and find a home that suits your needs because it may not be there if you wait too long.

Is This a Long Process?

This depends on you for the most part. If you are a picky person who has their heart set on a particular property type, then yes this will add to how long the process takes. If you have credit issues, or do not have the down payment or you are struggling to provide the necessary documentation the bank needs then your process will be hindered or stopped altogether.

To give a general answer this process can take anywhere from 30 to 120 days depending on your particular situation.

How Many Homes Should I View?

As many as you possibly need to, as long as they check off your "needs list" at the bare minimum. The reason for this is by seeing homes, even those that don't necessarily fit what you are looking for exactly, you get the opportunity to see first-hand some things that you may have wanted that just don't work in reality and you get to see some aspects of a home that work that you did not even know you wanted or needed. It is easier to commit to a home when you know what else is on the market.

What Should I Offer on the Property?

Make an offer that you will not regret later; meaning don't offer so much that you later have remorse about putting out so much money by acting in the moment, stay within your comfort level. On the other hand, don't offer so little that you lose the property you really wanted because you would not come up with an extra four or five thousand dollars; ultimately it depends on how much you value the property.

> **Quick Tip:** Do your homework when it comes to what the property will cost you because you might be amazed at how little an extra ten grand changes your monthly payment.

Inspections

To avoid any surprises or costly repairs later on it would be wise to get as many inspections as you can on the property; if it can be inspected then get it inspected (general inspection, plumbing, roofing, electrical, foundation, termite, sewer...etc.)

> **Quick Tip #1:** As a buyer you can possibly use the inspection reports to renegotiate your deal. You might spend around $2000 or more on inspections but save that money on the back end when you ask for a reasonable credit from the seller. Typically, at this point the seller is tired of showing the property, they have finally gotten an offer in and in many cases are "motivated" to close and move on from the property.
>
> **Quick Tip #2:** When you ask for a credit on repairs for a property do not itemize them and give it to the seller because they will sit down and mentally nitpick the list on what they feel the repairs should cost. Instead gather all of the reports that you have and simply tell the seller the total cost for repairs is "xyz" but you are only asking for "xyz" towards repairs on the property, and then you will close.

Costs to Prepare For

- Inspections can cost you anywhere from $300 to $3000 depending on what all you have inspected. Seems like a lot but generally can be negotiated off the purchase price or credited towards your closing costs.

- Any time you get a loan for a property the lender will require you to get an appraisal to ensure it is worth what you are actually buying it for. This can cost anywhere from $300 to $1000. While it's not normal depending on your relationship with the bank they may choose to waive this fee entirely.

- Banks will charge several direct fees (credit reporting, tax services, loan origination…etc.) This will vary by lender and the property price and type.

- Banks also tend to charge miscellaneous fees (notary, messenger fees, audit fee, recording fees…etc.)

  > **Quick Tip #1:** Shop around with your offer you may just get a better deal. Take offer one to your other bank and see if they can beat it, if they can (get it in writing) then take that back to the first bank and see if they will beat the offer. Sometimes they will but sometimes they will at least match the new offer. Take that offer to a third bank to see if they will beat it; do this until you get the best offer (your relationship with the bank helps this).

- Insurance must be paid up on the property when you close, typically the premium must be paid up for about six months to a year.

- Escrow fees are to ensure that both parties in the deal are compliant and doing things "by the book". This price will vary depending on the company, property price and type. Escrow companies, in some cases, will charge general fees whether or not you use them or not. Itemize anything that you do not utilize and ask the escrow company for a refund on these; it's not typical but sometimes these small fees do occur.

Quick Tip #2: Nothing is set in stone, when working a deal everything is negotiable; the worse they can do is say no.

- Title Fees are to ensure that the property is clean and clear of liens and encumbrances, and you can take legal full right of the property. These fees can range from $200 to $1100 (give or take) depending on the company and property.

Quick Tip #3: A lien is basically the legal rights over a property granted to an individual until an underlying obligation, usually a debt, is satisfied. An encumbrance, unlike a lien, does not prohibit the pass of title from one individual to the next, but it does to some extent devalue it. This can come in the form of deed restrictions, easements, encroachments and licenses…etc.

Quick Tip #4: When determining how much house you can truly afford, do not stop at the price the bank told you that you can afford monthly. This price does not account for other expenses that you will incur during ownership. Be mindful unlike an apartment, if and when something breaks, you will have to come out of pocket for it. Also, you have yearly property taxes, insurance premiums, general maintenance (broken appliances or roof repair), general upkeep (cutting the grass or power washing the house) and possible HOA payments.

Home Buying Self-Assessment

Take this time to identify your current situation. As you answer the following questions be honest, be detailed and even make itemized charts to organize your answers. This information will help you determine where you are currently and help you determine the steps needed to get where you want to be.

- Is buying a home the best option or would you be better off renting?
- Why do you want/need a home at this time?
- Do you have the necessary items to complete the process?
- Is your credit and income strong enough to purchase the home you want?
- Which loan type suits your needs best?
- Did you get pre-approved?
- Will you need a down payment? How much and do you currently have it?
- Do you have the funds available for other incurred costs of home buying?
- Do you have a financial institution willing to finance the home?
- Did you check the terms/rates of multiple financial institutions?
- Did you see if the others could match or beat the lowest deal you received?
- Did you decide to use an agent or not? Why?
- How many homes have you seen? Plan to see in total?

- What did you learn about your local housing market and about yourself?
- Do you need to sell a current house before closing on a new one?
- What inspections did/will you have done? How much will that cost?
- What area suits you best?
- What are your bottom-line must-haves in a home?
- What are your absolute deal breakers on a home?
- Can your budget handle the maintenance and upkeep of a home?
- Do you plan to live in the home long term or short term? Why?
- If short term, what is your future strategy for the home?

What is a Corporation Exactly?

Corporation

Honestly, a corporation is nothing more than a file of paperwork that is on record with your local governing body. Although many people often think of a brick-and-mortar building, advancements in technology make it possible to never have a building, and in some cases, never handle your own merchandise.

I have spoken a lot on having the proper foundation and here is no different. When you are considering starting a business, research the benefits, protections and how each corporation type handles taxes.

> Quick Tip: I believe in life you should never do anything without insurance. Meaning always protect yourself in any situation you go into; by choosing the right corporation structure you essentially set up an "insurance plan" for the future. There is no point in putting your blood, sweat and tears into something only to lose it all or give up your profits to heavy taxation.

There are several types of corporations, the following are just the most utilized and discussed. Also, rules and guidelines do change from time to time, so do your research, so you are aware of the current guidelines as well as how your state handles various corporation structure.

- **General Partnership:** Two or more people who come together to profit collectively in a business venture.

- **Sole Proprietorship:** A structure operated and owned by a single person and the business is not considered a separate entity.
- **Limited Liability Company (LLC):** This structure protects its owner(s) from personal responsibility of the entity's debts or liabilities.
- **Limited Liability Partnership (LLP):** Depending on the case a portion of, or all the partners have limited personal liability.
- **Limited Partnership:** Two or more partners joined together for business but only liable up to the extent of their contribution.
- **C Corporation:** Often called a "C-Corp", this structure is where the owners or shareholders are taxed separately.
- **S Corporation:** Often called a "S-Corp", this structure passes income, losses, deductions, and credits through to the shareholders.
- **Nonprofit Corporation:** Formed for the purpose of making profits for its owners or shareholders.
- **Nonprofit Organization:** Formed for the purpose of achieving a certain benefit and is not profit driven.
- Different States Offer Different Tax Advantages (Delaware, Wyoming, Nevada…etc.)

The Reality of it All

The discussion of corporations and all they entail is a lengthy discussion. A book could be written on each individual type. The factors that go into which corporation structure is best all depends on you, the type of business you plan to run, if you will have shareholders or ever plan to go public, do you want asset protection, what level of liability do you want, if you want the business to be its own entity, do you want to be taxed separate from your business and the list goes on and on.

The best way to determine which structure is best is to first research; yes, I could drag this on page after page detailing each corporation structure but most of it would probably not even apply to what you plan to do. To save time, think of a few advantages and benefits you want in your structure and determine which structures offer that. If you are truly serious about this, go sit and talk with a professional so that you can detail what benefits are important to you and they can not only lead you in the right direction but also introduce you to some added benefits you may not have known.

Some of this may cost you time and money but if you are not willing to invest into yourself and the future of your business then you may want to reconsider it all together. As well, some of the relationships you form with these professionals early on may be useful down the road. Wealthy people understand the importance of a good team and the plethora of knowledge and insight they bring.

In addition to the corporation structure, you choose it is important to research and understand what additional tax benefits certain states may offer. Again, there are so many variances here it would take another book to detail them all. You would be amazed at the amount of people who start a corporation in a certain state just to avoid taxes on their new Lamborghini or Ferrari; yes, this is actually a thing.

> **Quick Tip #1:** The top four corporation structures that protect your assets and limit your liability are Limited Liability Companies (LLCs), Limited Partnerships (LPs), S Corporations and C Corporations. Everyone is different and not everyone plans to have a ton of assets so as I continue to say, do your research and see what fits your plans.
>
> **Quick Tip #2:** When you hear the phrase nonprofit corporation, or organization, this does not mean they do not make a profit. In fact, some nonprofit organizations bring in millions of dollars each year. In addition, nonprofit structures like the 501(c)(3) are exempt from federal income tax and they can avoid paying property taxes.

This section is to encourage you to really delve into all the possibilities of corporations and how they can benefit you long term. Once you understand all the loopholes and incentives it is easier to see that rich people, wealthy people, financially free people (whatever you call them) aren't as evil as many people think. In reality, they have made educational investments in themselves, so they understand how to build their wealth and keep more of it along the way. It's not some secret hidden in a vault, you just have to take time out and get an understanding of how to play the game of corporations.

> **Quick Tip #3:** When deciding on what corporation structure suits your business best you can sometimes simply research other major players in your field and see what structures they operate from, if it isn't broken don't fix it.

Corporation Self-Assessment

Take this time to identify your current situation. As you answer the following questions be honest, be detailed and even make itemized charts to organize your answers. This information will help you determine where you are currently and help you determine the steps needed to get where you want to be.

- Have you determined what corporation structure suits you best?
- How much time did you spend looking into the pros and cons of each?
- What are your top two options? Why?
- What corporation benefits fit your needs most?
- What are the tax benefits?
- How does the structure you chose handle liability?
- Will you be going into business alone or with others?
- Is this a temporary corporation or one that will run perpetually?
- Will you issue stock and have shareholders?
- Is your corporation a for-profit or a non-profit?
- Do you have the necessary forms and paperwork to file?
- Where is the local office where you file this paperwork?
- What are the fees they charge?
- Is there a notary available at your financial institution?
- Will your corporation be the parent company to other subsidiaries?

Basics of Starting a Business

From the Ground Floor

As discussed in the corporation section, there are many benefits, protections, tax benefits depending on what corporation type you choose. These benefits are why the wealthy and financially free choose to have assets instead of simply working a job for pay. This is not to say you can't do both, but the assets just ensure no one can put a cap on how much you make, and they ensure taxes do not eat up your profits as they increase.

Where to Start?

Because of technological advances and various social media platforms you now have the traditional way of starting a business and what I like to call the tech-age way of starting a business. There are many similarities, the order of them is what really differentiates the two.

You often hear people talk about a business plan. The purpose of this is because it will, in detail, answer many questions you may have or that a lender may have. I encourage you to determine whether or not this will be beneficial in starting your business. Can you start a successful business without one of these? Yes you can but most of the information you may want can be answered here.

In this plan you want to detail the following (or more depending on your situation):

- Company Name: This is critical because it can be the difference between reaching only a particular segment or having something that can reach a broad target market. (If you plan to sale more than just coats then do not put "coat factory" in your name only to spend a ton of money down the road on marketing and rebranding your company)

- Company Branding (logo, colors, graphics…etc.)
- Mission Statement or Vision Statement (clarifies the core values of your company)
- Company Overview: Detail why the business venture will succeed. You can include a S.W.O.T (Strengths, Weaknesses, Opportunities & Threats) analysis here which identifies the strengths, weaknesses, opportunities, and threats for your business.
- What goods or services you plan to offer: Detail how your goods or services benefit current customers (if you have them) and how they will benefit potential customers. Here you also want to include product costs to you and the customer as well as possible supplies and other companies involved that will help with the process.
- Your Target Market
- Statistics that identify a need for those goods or services (internet research)
- Statistics that support the chosen target market (internet research)
- Identification and evaluation of competition: Pay close attention here because these are the businesses that you will have to compete with either directly or indirectly. This means if you want to open a bakery then other bakeries, and grocery stores with a bakery department, are your direct competition. Other companies that have goods or services that are not the same as yours but could still meet the needs of your customers are indirect competition. Researching your competitors and doing a S.W.O.T analysis, can allow you to identify what makes your competition work well so you know what keeps attracting customers. Additionally, you will be able to identify exploitable

weaknesses to create a better system. There are plenty of companies that sell chicken nuggets and chicken sandwiches but only a few are able to handle increased demand because their system is better, plain and simple.

- Management and Organization: In this section you detail the ownership of the company, the management, and board of directors if it applies. Detail who will do what and list out their experience, qualifications, and education as it pertains to your business and their duties.

- Marketing and Sales: Detail how you plan to penetrate the market, so your target market knows who you are and what you do or offer. Additionally, you want to detail how you plan to drive sales, your growth strategy (how you plan to grow and how you plan to handle the growth), and what possible sales activities and actions will be implemented.

- Funding Requirements: Here you must determine all the possible cost associated with your business so that you can come up with immediate, short -range and long-range strategies to accommodate and handle these costs. If you can't afford the product there will be nothing to sell and if you can't afford employees, then no services can be rendered. Additionally, if you plan to get a loan of some sort a financial institution wants to see where the requested funds will be going, how you plan to pay them back, if you have done your homework and have realistic figures that are justified and if your business is sustainable and worth the risk.

> **Quick Tip:** Don't be overwhelmed, anything worth having is worth the work to make it happen. This goes back to laying the proper foundation now for the type of results you want later. Also, this is you further investing in not only yourself but also your business. Going the extra mile will have you better prepared for what's to come; this is not an overnight process.

Forms and Filings

There are a ton of possible forms that you may come across when you start the incorporation process. There are name reserve forms, name change forms, articles of incorporation forms, articles of organization forms and the list goes on.

When dealing with these there are several people that will sell you the forms for a fee, however you can get them online for free or go to your local probate court, secretary of state website, filing department or whatever they have chosen to label it in your state. To get details on forms, where to go to file them and associated fees every state has their own website where you can find a "corporations" section.

Filling these forms out is a pretty simple task, however if you do need additional help with the wording or what exactly they want, again don't pay someone just go to the local office and they will walk you through for free. As well, depending on the corporation type you chose they will even direct you to the right forms and what steps are necessary to complete the paperwork. While help is available to you, remember this is your business you want to research and learn along the way so that you at least have a basic understanding of what is going on because not everyone has your best interest at hand and not everyone is willing to help even if it's their job.

> **Quick Tip #1:** Many of these forms come with various fees so make sure you know everything you have to pay for before you are about to do the final submission. As well, there are certain things you may have to mail so have some envelopes and stamps ready because every item you prepare for helps the process move that much fast.
>
> **Quick Tip #2:** At the end of the incorporation process you will need to file a SS-4 Form with the IRS in order to obtain your Employer Identification Number (referred to as an EIN). Once again, there are companies that will charge you $75 to as much as $300 to file this for you but you can file it for free on the IRS website and print out an official EIN at home. (The EIN acts as the social security number of your corporation because it is considered a separate entity, essentially another person).

> **Quick Tip #3:** Some businesses require certain forms, filings, permits… etc that others do not. For example, if you plan to serve food and drinks now you need a food permit, possibly a license to sell alcohol, the health department gets involved, and even how you handle your business license comes into play. This will vary by business, by the market the business is in, and if the business is fully online, traditional brick and mortar or a combination of the two; so be proactive and ask questions that's why the people are there.
>
> **Advanced Quick Tip:** Your company will have credit and although it does not work the same as your personal credit file you want to make sure it stays positive because it is possible for your company to purchase your home, cars and other items which comes with an array of benefits, and protections in case of a lawsuit. Learning the basics is important so you can enjoy the many benefits available down the road.

Articles of Incorporation

This documentation establishes a corporation as a separate business entity. These articles are public record and provide pertinent information about the corporation to the public. This can typically be done by submitting a designated form or by having them typed up, signed and notarized.

> **Quick Tip:** If ever you need something notarized go to the financial institution where you have an account, and they should have someone on staff who will do it for free; make sure you have the proper identification present.

The following should be included in your "detailed" articles:

- Your company name and the principal office address
- The purpose of your corporation (depending on your state you may be allowed to provide a general purpose)

- The duration of your corporation (most commonly people intend for their corporation to exist perpetually, however in some cases the corporation only needs to exist for a limited time frame.

- The name and address of the registered agent and registered office (a registered agent is a physical person who acts on behalf of the corporation to handle documentation and lawsuits. Some states require that a document agreeing to act as an agent must be signed)

- The initial board of directors (president, vice president, treasurer...etc.) (some states will require the names and addresses of these members).

- If you plan to issue stock, then you must detail the number and type of shares of stock the corporation is authorized to issue. (This number may be used to calculate applicable taxes and fees)

- The names and addresses of the incorporators (An incorporator is a person who handles the articles being filed and signs them. This person does not have to be a shareholder, officer, or director of the corporation; the corporation can have multiple incorporators)

- Bylaws: an account of how the corporate members will be governed (rules) and how (if at all) those rules can be amended, altered, or rescinded.

- Dissolution: This deals with what will happen to the assets, funds, and other items in the event the corporation is terminated.

- Proper signatures of incorporators and an authorized notary signature and seal.

Traditional or Tech-Age?

The only key difference between these two is the order in which you do things and with the internet you can reach a broader audience and do much of your marketing and advertising for free. Today there are more options on how you get your products to customers and more effective ways to provide services. The advancements of today allow you to take your idea to the next level or reinvent an old one. For example, taxis were great when they first came on the scene, but with the emergence of apps like Uber and Lyft the service offered isn't a new concept but the way we go about it now is. The post office revolutionized the way we send mail, companies like FedEx and UPS took things to the next level but Amazon and their prime shipping options have taken a traditional way of doing things and taken it to yet another level.

The traditional way of doing business required you to do a business plan and submit it to obtain funding and while many financial institutions still require it today there are a ton of new ways to get funding (a lot of people today do what is called crowdfunding or hard money lending). There is no sure way to determine and prepare for everything in the world of business so don't let the process make you quit; set the foundation and jump into what you want to do.

> **Quick Tip:** Understand there is a big difference between education and schooling. I have several degrees, including one in business, but school does not teach you how to start a company, they teach you how to work for one. There are still some benefits to a formal education because you will still need to at least know the basics of accounting, finance and so on to understand what is going on even if you are paying a professional.

I mention education and other aspects because as you journey towards starting a business, just like in previous sections, the company you keep matters. You can't let people persuade you to not follow your dreams. People will give you every reason not to start a business and they will also give you a long list of things they claim you need all the while they have never started a business and have no idea.

When it comes to your idea do not just write off ideas as stupid, automatically think you will not succeed or let people detour you from your dreams because they don't consider your business idea a good one and here's why:

- In 1975 Gary Dahl had the idea to sell rocks; yes rocks. He drew little faces on the rocks and pitched them to parents as pets for their kids. He explained that there is no clean up or up-keep for these pets and they would never die but be around for years to give their children comfort. Gary made $15 million dollars from this idea.

- Samantha Hess created a professional cuddling service that was bringing in around $50k annually back in 2014; her certification classes started at $900 to become a professional cuddle buddy.

- Robert Samuel started a professional line sitter business where you pay people to stand in long lines for you which brought in around $60k annually.

- Jenn and Phil Tompkins made over $200,000 dollars on their rent a chicken business for people who want a chicken and fresh eggs but only for a limited time.

- Josh Opperman raked in $15 million dollars in profits in 2015. After his fiancée left him, he started a business where people could resale their rings to new couples.

- Moses Lam and Troy Paquette started vitality air. They bring in around $300,000 annually by selling bottles of air; no, you didn't read that wrong. China is covered in smog so they got the idea to sell a breath of fresh air to them with the idea that if they can import food and other necessities, they have the right to import fresh air from Canada.

- The next time someone questions your business idea be sure to rattle off a few of these figures. In today's society just about anything is possible so trust the process and believe in yourself even if no one else does. Also, don't be your own worst enemy, get out of your own head. If you don't believe in you and your product then no one else will either.

- In a previous section I discussed the power of no and here isn't any different. The list of people who failed or were told no include Walt Disney, Oprah, Steven Spielberg, Albert Einstein, and even Theodor Seuss Geisel better known as Dr. Seuss. Whether you are giving the no or receiving it, use it for your benefit, allow it to further fuel your ambition towards success. If these, and many others like them, had just given up at the first no just think of all the things they would've never achieved.

- Don't let age be a reason not to go after your dreams. Viola Davis, Samuel L Jackson, Henry Ford and Colonel Sanders all became successful later in life. Keep this in mind if someone wants to claim you're too old or waited too late in life to get started. Most importantly remind yourself it's not too late.

What's Next?

I have mentioned being prepared and being ready; the fact of the matter is you will never be one hundred percent ready so do not use this as an excuse to not get started with your business. Yes, there are risks associated with starting a business but looking at the current state of the job market there is definitely a fair share of risk involved there as well.

> **Quick Tip #1:** KNOW YOUR MARKET...What I mean here is you need to understand what your consumers want and what price points fit in the market you are operating in.

I have gone over similarities and differences between starting a business traditionally and starting one in the tech-age. Most of the paperwork remains the same and guidelines vary a little. With a traditional business you had to open your doors first, then build your brand, build up customers and get your product out to the people while maintaining your reputation, or brand. With the tech-age approach to business many people build their brand first before ever offering a product or service; this is what I meant by doing things in a different order.

Plenty of people have used Instagram, Facebook, Twitter, Snapchat and so on to build a solid brand with a solid following. After this you may notice they start selling something, or advertising a service, or making money from advertising for others. This is the new way that a lot of businesses are getting started because essentially you get the customers before ever offering them anything.

As you go through the steps of starting a business by now you have figured out the product or service you would like to offer and in business, we would say you have found your niche. To put this in social media terms this is what people do when they use hashtags on Instagram. If you want people who are excited about make-up, clothing, or natural hair to see what you are doing then the hashtag allows you to broadcast to that niche of people.

While building your brand ensure that you are increasing your presence through social media, possibly a website, but do not forget search engine optimization (SEO). Your brand means nothing if people do not know about it so the more it is before potential customers the more people you will gain. Search engines like Google and Yahoo are often used to find businesses. To take better advantage of this you want your webpage, social media pages and so on to answer as many of the questions that people searching may have. That way you come up as an option more than others that may only be answering limited items. Therefore people who have a strong social media presence from videos also choose to do blogs discussing the same content because the internet can easily find wording when someone does a search, thus increasing your exposure.

When using social media to grow your brand and increase the number of people who know about you make sure that you are actively interacting with other pages so that more people will be prone to check out what you are doing because you have similar interests (interacting on social media helps with the algorithm and in turn helps with exposure)

When it comes to your webpage, blogs, social media platforms and other outlets you are using, be sure that you are giving people a reason to not only investigate what you are doing but also stick around for more. I previously spoke on getting the greatest benefit or value from your credit cards; well, your potential customers should get the same feeling when they come into contact with your outlets.

People typically follow things that incite emotions, they find entertaining, or it educates them on something they are already interested in. Therefore people follow pages that educate them on how to do the things they love, comedic pages that constantly post content they find funny and pages that shine light on social injustice or unfair treatment of people or animals.

> **Quick Tip #2:** You need to establish a direct line of communication between you, your current customers, and potential customers. A great way to do this is to give them something for free by email. They get something for free, and you now have their email address for use in the future so whether they revisit your webpage or

social media platforms again you have access to them. If you plan on selling a recipe book, give away a free mini e-book with some simple recipes, if you are going to do a make-up line you could send a free tutorial video so customers can see the product in action. No matter what you are doing there is a way to express value to customers while giving them something free and obtaining their email addresses. If social media were to shut down or they decided to change their algorithms, like YouTube does, then your audience changes and you may lose potential customers.

Quick Tip #3: Once you get to the point of selling an actual product, do not be afraid to pay commission to people who can get your product out even more. There are certain people who have a different following than you, they run in different circles than you do so they come across people you may never run into otherwise. This not only broadens your reach, but it also puts some of the load on someone else while still getting your product out. If you choose to post pictures of your merchandise, be mindful people get bored easily so find creative ways to showcase your products. Whether you sell shoes, clothes, or some innovative gadget you created; showcase nice photos and videos of people actually wearing or utilizing your product this will have a great effect and get people's attention better.

Business Start-Up Self-Assessment

Take this time to identify your current situation. As you answer the following questions be honest, be detailed and even make itemized charts to organize your answers. This information will help you determine where you are currently and help you determine the steps needed to get where you want to be.

- Why do you want to start a business?
- What type of business do you want to start?
- What goods or services will be offered?
- What is the name of your business?
- What does this name say about your business?
- Does this start-up require a business plan?
- Did you map out a business plan to see where you stand currently?
- What did you learn?
- What will differentiate your business from others?
- Define your management structure; who will do what?
- Do you currently have potential customers? How will you gain more?
- What are the funding requirements in order to make your vision a reality?
- Have you filed all the necessary paperwork and paid your fees?
- Do you have an EIN?
- Do you have a business bank account?

- Will your business be online, have a physical building, or both? Why?
- Who is your direct/indirect competition?
- Who is your target market?
- Is there a need for your product or service within that market?
- Do you have an established brand, or do you need to build one?
- What steps will you take to positively build your brand?
- What outlets will you use to inform the public about your business?
- Do you have a person handling your taxes that understands business taxation

Sneak peek into

MONEY MATTERS & FINANCIAL EDUCATION

WHAT THEY NEVER TAUGHT YOU IN SCHOOL!

BOOK II

In Book Two I'll delve into....

- How to make money with your credit
- Strategies to travel the world completely free
- Getting the latest technology without spending a dime of your own money
- How to get more value out of your credit cards and offset your annual fees
- Building business credit with Dun & Bradstreet, Experian, and Equifax
- Business credit cards and business lines of credit
- How to advance from one business vendor tier to another
- Why business credit cards are even better than personal cards
- Real estate investing basics (house hacking, wholesaling, corporate leasing, brrrr method)
- The importance of life insurance, trusts and holding companies
- How to properly structure your business to mitigate taxes
- How to gain more real estate without any money down
- How to improve your personal debt to income ratio by utilizing your business credit.
- Purchasing a car in your business name with no money out of pocket
- Purchasing your personal home or investment property in your business name

About the Author

RALPH CARMICHAEL II, M.Ed., is an Alabama native and a graduate of Murphy High School. He thrives on helping individuals transform their lives in business as well as real estate. His dedication to the field of business has led him to being a triple alumnus from the University of South Alabama with degrees ranging from Entrepreneurial Business Management, Public Relations, and Advertising, as well as a Master's in Higher Educational Administration. He has mentored many young adults on topics relating to establishing credit, business development, and money management.

While having established a firm foundation in the field of education and business, his passion to reach young leaders of tomorrow is ever present. He has spoken to various faith-based organizations, helping to engage audiences on self-improvement and the foundational learning of financial literacy. With well over two decades of experience, Ralph Carmichael II has used his expertise to help others develop successful businesses, discover how to make their money work for them, and develop the skills necessary to help them maintain more of the revenues they generate.

He has an extensive portfolio that encompasses a lucrative real estate company, an academy shaping the young minds of tomorrow, and other businesses in which he is a silent partner. He also owns, manages, and oversees numerous rental properties, lands, and the development of commercial real estate across multiple states. In his spare time Ralph Carmichael II enjoys traveling the world, photographing unique architecture and being a connoisseur of fine foods.

Made in the USA
Monee, IL
04 November 2026

67382713R10069